WHEN
DESIGN
REALLY
WORKS

A Quintessence Book

This edition for the United States and Canada published in 2014
by Barron's Educational Series, Inc.

Copyright © 2014 Quintessence Editions Ltd.

All inquiries should be addressed to:
Barron's Educational Series, Inc.
250 Wireless Boulevard
Hauppauge, New York 11788
www.barronseduc.com

ISBN: 978-1-4380-0454-9

Library of Congress Control No. 2013955799

This book was designed and produced by
Quintessence Editions Ltd.
The Old Brewery, 6 Blundell Street, London, N7 9BH

Project Editor	Becky Gee
Editor	Helen Coultas
Designers	Tom Howey, Christine Lacey
Editorial Assistant	Zoë Smith
Editorial Director	Jane Laing
Publisher	Mark Fletcher

Color separation by KHL Chromagraphics, Singapore
Printed by 1010 Printing International Limited, China

9 8 7 6 5 4 3 2 1

FRONT COVER: Red and Blue Chair, Gerrit Rietveld, 1918

BACK COVER:
Arco Lamp, Achille and Pier Giacomo Castiglioni, 1962

Susie Hodge

WHEN DESIGN REALLY WORKS

BARRON'S

CONTENTS

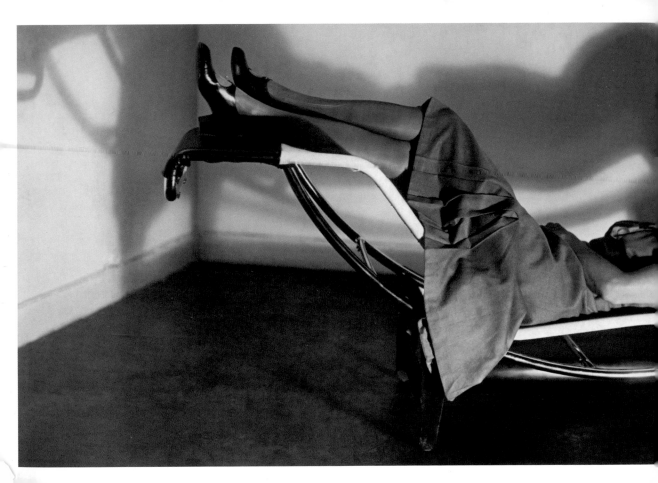

INTRODUCTION

Designs—and so designers—have enormous influence. From furniture to fabrics, containers to cameras, glassware to gadgets, every man-made object has been designed by someone and affects the user directly. But what makes a great design? Can there ever be agreed criteria? Many people have strong opinions on what good design looks like, how it works, and what materials should be used in its making. Assessments and conclusions are as varied as the designs themselves. In general, a successful design is versatile and practical; it functions exceptionally well, looks good, and is reasonably priced. Naturally, most designers strive to achieve exactly these qualities, but some designs are not always as excellent as the designer intended. Many beautiful designs have been produced, and many well-functioning ones, but not all are one and the same. Great design is when everything—particularly form and function—comes together in one object that fulfills its purpose in every way.

Design is a major part of a society's culture because it shapes the ways in which we live and work. Our appreciation of whether a design really works is affected by many factors, including our culture, background, surroundings, perceptions, age, nationality, and race, as well as by

any personal knowledge of the elements that go into making a design aesthetically functional. Some designs attain a cultural significance as time passes, whereas others can be diminished by changing outlooks or political situations.

Although objects such as the wheel, the pestle and mortar, and the quill were designed centuries ago, the profession of designer as we know it began to develop only in the eighteenth century, as a direct result of the Industrial Revolution. Previously, there were inventors and craftsmen, who produced items to assist the smooth functioning of society. The technological advances that occurred during the Industrial Revolution allowed a large variety of goods to be manufactured that were affordable to ordinary people for the first time. Machines were used to mass-produce objects and, concurrently, the middle classes became increasingly wealthy. The need to meet the growing demand for man-made items and consumer goods led to manufacturers employing people to draw and plan products. By the nineteenth century, further new inventions, technologies, materials, and techniques had an immense impact on every aspect of human life, and the profession of designer became even more specialized.

A number of new designers opposed mass-production but many embraced it. Some relished the challenge of working with new materials and production methods, which gave them scope to create innovative items and a chance to sell countless versions of one design. Others looked back to the pre-industrial era, drawing inspiration from traditional shapes and materials, and finding beauty in the natural world and handcrafted goods. From the nineteenth to the twentieth centuries, productive partnerships between designers and manufacturers resulted in many original designs. As consumer demands gathered momentum, further new inventions and designs were produced. The market became particularly competitive, pushing designers to be ever more creative and innovative.

The test of time sets apart a good design, and many of the best ones continue to be used decades after they were first produced. Some, such as the safety pin by Walter Hunt, Le Parfait jars, and the automatic tape measure by James Chesterman, have never been bettered. Technological advances inevitably make an impact, and what was once a brilliant design can fall out of favor, either because new inventions and technologies have forced it to become obsolete, or because its shapes, materials, and form appear dated. When designs really work, they are admired for the timelessness of their construction, function, and aesthetic appeal.

When Design Really Works considers eighty of the best designs, from the late eighteenth to the twenty-first centuries. The selection includes a

Tulip and Rose Fabric (1876)
William Morris
≫ BEAUTY p.21

Peony Tiffany Lamp (c. 1915)
Louis Comfort Tiffany
≫ BEAUTY p.29

wide range of objects: from pens, stools, and coffee machines, to vases, watches, and lamps. They are mostly versatile and iconic products, and often classics of the past and of the future. The designers who created them are from diverse backgrounds: born in different eras and countries, they have experienced vastly differing cultural, social, and political situations, and have worked with a variety of briefs, considerations, and budgets. Their target consumers are equally diverse. Some of the most iconic designs have been developed by designers who have pushed the materials or production methods beyond accepted boundaries: they may have been irreverent toward the past, or simply audacious in their approach.

Each design in this book has been chosen for its originality, appearance, form, materials, and function. Diversity, creativity, and invention have all been celebrated. A number of designs have also been selected for their longevity, popularity, and versatility, and most for being the first of their kind. Some of the items, such as Wilhelm Wagenfeld's glass tea set, the model LC4 chaise longue by Le Corbusier, Pierre Jeanneret, and Charlotte Perriand, and the KitchenAid food mixer by Egmont Arens, have remained aesthetically appealing since they were first designed, despite countless imitations and newer technologies threatening to supplant them. The book considers the balance of invention over design, and, likewise, of aesthetics

Swatch Watch (1983)
Swatch
⬦ FUNCTION p.87

over function. When does invention or beauty take precedence over design? And should this matter? Usefulness is also assessed. Although some designs can be seen as purely functional, including the Montblanc pen, Cesca chair, and Swatch watch, others, such as the Savoy vase and Fabergé egg, are almost entirely decorative. These items, made predominantly to adorn a space, can be designed more freely than objects such as cutlery and cookware, in which form has to follow function. But do these restrictions make a difference to the greatness of a design?

The eighty designs have been categorized into ten themed chapters: Beauty, Individuality, Form, Function, Expression, Movement, Impact, Convenience, Communication, and Harmony. Eight designs feature in each chapter: for example, the Bacchantes vase by René Lalique and a Chinoiserie cupboard by Thomas Chippendale are in the chapter on Beauty; the fluid S chair by Verner Panton and Coco Chanel's geometric No. 5 perfume bottle are included in Form; Harry Beck's systematic London Underground map is in the Convenience chapter, and the contoured glass Coca-Cola bottle by Earl R. Dean is featured in Harmony. The book is not a chronological history of design, nor are the designs grouped into types of products, eras, movements, or materials. Each design's placement in the book is determined by its style and structure.

Within the chapters, entries are categorized by a sub-theme. These define the reason why the individual designs have worked so well, and describe the essence of each one. For example, Christopher Dresser's sleek soup tureen and ladle are in the chapter on Beauty, and analyzed under the sub-theme "Grace." Similarly, in the chapter on Communication, Maija Isola's vibrant and bold Unikko fabric is considered for its "Courage," whereas in the Function chapter, Edwin H. Land's Polaroid camera is examined in terms of "Immediacy." In this way, the designs are investigated on several different levels, thereby providing a comprehensive and extensive appraisal.

Throughout *When Design Really Works*, you will discover why the designers created their particular products when they did, how each designer worked, which materials they used, and how the objects were received by contemporary consumers. The book also gives examples of other similar designs and brief biographies of the designers. Images featured include many in-context photographs, which convey the cultural significance of the design, plus either a particular detail of a design or an earlier or later model, all intended to provide a clearer appreciation of the designers' thought processes and resolutions.

Successful design is much more than being fashionable and functional. It is an inherent understanding, by each designer, of materials and

Polaroid Land Camera
Model 95 (1948)
Edwin H. Land
⊠ FUNCTION p.85

Barcelona Chair (c. 1929)
**Ludwig Mies van der Rohe
and Lilly Reich**
⊠ HARMONY p.183

processes, and a clear vision of how the product will be used. A number of designers take years to achieve greatness in one product, because they are determined to devise methods or to manipulate materials in original and practical ways. Some succeed in their endeavors, whereas others abandon the task and go on to design something completely different. Several designers have unwittingly discovered innovative techniques or uses of certain materials, whereas others, such as Dieter Rams and Michael Graves, have consistently produced a varied range of inventive, effective, and avant-garde products. Not all designers have attained fame and fortune from their designs, and some remain virtually unknown.

Designers are not confined to a single field of expertise and may produce exemplary designs in a number of different areas. Karl Elsener originally designed surgical equipment before producing the iconic Swiss army knife, and Ludwig Mies van der Rohe was recognized as a successful architect before his Barcelona chair was hailed as one of the greatest furniture designs of the twentieth century. Not all of the individuals featured in *When Design Really Works* were designers by trade. Some simply had a knack for it, such as mechanic Walter Hunt, who, in addition to the safety pin, designed a street-sweeping machine, sewing machine, fountain pen, flax-spinner, and several other household items. Other designers, such

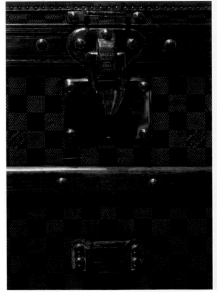

as Ernö Rubik and Chuck Taylor, have produced a single groundbreaking design with which their name has become synonymous worldwide.

The most innovative, beautiful, and influential designs have often developed from prevailing social, cultural, or political influences, such as art movements, new technologies, and the two World Wars. For example, although the Minimalist design style is different from the art movement's philosophies, the simple contours and limited colors of Minimalism emerged in design from fine art experiments, and the style was particularly popular during the 1980s. Modernism was another powerful influence on both art and design, with similar philosophies but different outcomes. Modernist artists and designers rejected the past and created new things to endorse the industrialized world. In fine art, this resulted in abstract paintings, while designers produced objects with clean, angular, or smooth lines and surfaces. Additionally, different nations have made particular contributions to design. German designers, for example, have tended toward functionalism, whereas Italian designers have generally been more flamboyant and colorful. Scandinavian designers traditionally exploited their indigenous crafts and materials, while U.S. designers, particularly of the twentieth century, embraced such things as machines and Pop art, appealing directly to consumers and the expanding commercial world.

Designers today use a greater range of materials and production methods than ever before. Manufacturing processes have enabled them to create more designs to meet increasing consumer demands. Despite the technological advances, however, the principles of design remain the same as they always have been. Designers analyze the requirements of potential users, seek dexterous solutions, and produce attractive, practical, desirable, and affordable objects. This is the same approach that was taken by Josiah Wedgwood and Thomas Chippendale in the eighteenth century, by Michael Thonet and Louis Vuitton in the nineteenth century, and by Jonathan Ive and Tom Dixon in the twenty-first.

Every object in this book has been chosen for successfully combining technology, ergonomics, and aesthetics. Each one began as an idea, prompted by desire, ambition, or even frustration. And, when a design really works, it does what it was designed to do — beautifully and without fuss.

Susie Hodge

iPhone (2007)
Jonathan Ive
[»] FORM p.69

BEAUTY

> "A chair is a very difficult object. A skyscraper is almost easier. That is why Chippendale is famous."

Ludwig Mies van der Rohe architect

Softwood, paint. The delicate, fanciful style is typical of chinoiserie.

Corner Cupboard 1768–1778
Thomas Chippendale

At a time when there was a growing demand for luxury goods, Thomas Chippendale attracted to his fashionable London workshop numerous wealthy clients, who appreciated his beautifully produced furniture made with high-quality materials. In 1754, he became the first cabinetmaker to publish a book of his designs, with advice on color, textiles, and soft furnishings, titled *The Gentleman and Cabinet-Maker's Director*. His main influences were Chinese, Gothic, and French Rococo styles, and in this cabinet he blends delicate and fanciful oriental forms with the lightness and harmony of the Rococo.

Chippendale designed this elegant chinoiserie cabinet for his friend and patron, actor David Garrick. It is known as an encoignure (literally, the angle where two walls meet), which is a type of furniture that is specifically made for the corner of a room. Following contemporary reactions against the heavy formality of Baroque furniture, the refined, bow-fronted corner cupboard was part of a suite that Chippendale made for Garrick's bedroom, and such cabinets were usually made in pairs. The sinuous, asymmetrical design in soft green incorporates foliage, a bird, figures, and pagodas; it was painted to emulate Chinese wallpaper, which was popular at the time.

Ribbon-back Chair	Chinese Lacquer Secretaire	Four-seater Sofa	Cylinder Desk
Thomas Chippendale	**Thomas Chippendale**	**George Hepplewhite**	**Thomas Sheraton**
1754	c.1773	1788	1792

 William Morris was one of the main proponents of the Arts and Crafts Movement and the most influential designer of the nineteenth century. Enthused by every aspect of the arts, he based his original designs on nature, and changed how people decorated their homes. In 1875, he founded Morris & Co., with artists Edward Burne-Jones and Dante Gabriel Rossetti, to manufacture stained glass, murals, furniture, tiles, metal- and glassware, textiles and wallpapers, carpets, embroideries, and tapestries. Each piece was handmade using pre-Industrial Revolution processes. With its large rose and tulip petals, this woven fabric was one of Morris's many designs that helped to inspire the organic stylization of Art Nouveau.

 Woven woolen triple cloth, vegetable dyes. Morris disliked flat designs that "pretended" to be 3D, preferring to use flat lines and colors.

Tulip and Rose Fabric 1876
William Morris

> *Have nothing in your house that you do not know to be useful, or believe to be beautiful"*
>
> **William Morris**

In 1887, Morris designed Willow Bough (left) as wallpaper, and in about 1895 he produced it as a fabric, too. Fascinated by the natural world and the Middle Ages, he sourced his design ideas from gardens and country walks, as well as from woodcuts, illuminated manuscripts, and tapestries. He declared that patterns should have "unmistakable suggestions of gardens and fields." Shunning mechanical processes, he revived several crafts, including block printing, vegetable dyeing, and weaving. This print of sinuous willow branches and leaves was created with blocks of fine-grained pearwood. Like Tulip and Rose (opposite), it appears to be curving and liberated.

Acanthus Fabric
William Morris
1875

Honeysuckle Wallpaper
May Morris
1883

Birds Sateen Fabric
C. F. A. Voysey
c. 1893

Tulip Furnishing Fabric
John Henry Dearle
1900

Tureen and Ladle c. 1880
Christopher Dresser

The apparent simplicity of Dresser's shiny, curved soup tureen and ladle demonstrates his admiration for Japanese metalwork and the reduced shapes of Eastern design. Concentrating on graceful contours, he made versions of the two objects in both silver and electroplate, with either ebony or ivory handles. Streamlined and minimalist, they appear startlingly modern. The tureen's angular, oblique feet (left) emphasize the clean lines and assist its practicality: when full of hot soup, the bowl hovers above the surface on which it is placed.

Rejecting the prevailing ornate and embellished Victorian styles, Christopher Dresser embraced modern manufacturing methods with his designs for wallpaper, textiles, ceramics, furniture, and metalware. One of the first independent industrial designers of the late nineteenth century, he created objects that were elegant and beautiful as well as functional. This tureen and ladle show the influence of objects he saw during his four-month trip to Japan in 1876 to 1877 and demonstrate his unique blending of Japanese, ancient Egyptian, and Asian styles. Dresser maintained his belief in the supremacy of form over ornament and was one of the most versatile designers of his day.

> The beautiful must be truthful in expression, and graceful, delicate, and refined in contour, manifesting no coarseness, vulgarity, or obtrusiveness."
> **Christopher Dresser**

Electroplate with ebony handles. Dresser patented the tureen and ladle on July 28, 1880.

Shibayama Teapot
Christopher Dresser
1878–1879

Covered Tureen
Dominick & Haff
1881

Soup Tureen with Lid
Josef Hoffmann
1908

Hill House Ladder Back Chair 1903
Charles Rennie Mackintosh

Designed to enhance the white walls of the Hill House bedroom, Mackintosh's elegant ladder back chair contrasted with the spatial proportions of the room, while its darkened wood dramatically offset the white closets on either side (left). Following Mackintosh's belief that design comes before function, the rigid, masculine form of the chair also counterbalanced the surrounding, essentially feminine space. The confidently poised chair is characterized by an economy of line, while the grid pattern at the top is echoed elsewhere in the room.

At a time when popular tastes favored the curving lines of Art Nouveau, Charles Rennie Mackintosh created this distinctly rectilinear chair, demonstrating his modernist inclinations. Named after Hill House in Helensburgh, Scotland, which he designed for publisher Walter Blackie and his family, the chair was one of two made specifically for the main bedroom. Straight lines echo elements of the Vienna Secessionists and also of linear Japanese ideals of beauty that Mackintosh admired, but although every aspect appears straight, the back rungs curve slightly for comfort. The timber frame was ebonized to resemble lacquered wood used in Japanese furniture.

> "Life is the leaves which shape and nourish a plant, but 'art' is the flower which embodies its meaning."
>
> Charles Rennie McIntosh

Ebonized ashwood, sea grass fabric, horsehair.

+ Argyle Chair
Charles Rennie Mackintosh 1898–1899

Reclining Chair
Henry van de Velde
1903–1904

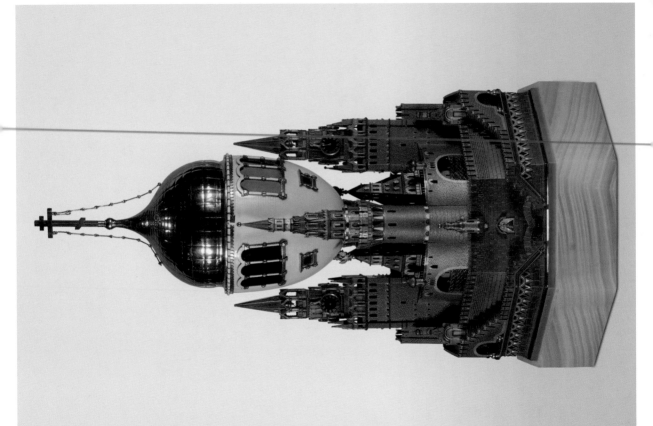

Moscow Kremlin Fabergé Egg 1906
Peter Carl Fabergé

The extravagant Alexander Palace Egg (left) was made in 1908 by Henrik Wigström, under Fabergé's direction, as a gift from Czar Nicholas II to his wife, Alexandra. It features miniature watercolor portraits of the imperial children: Olga, Tatiana, Maria, Anastasia, and Alexei. Above the portraits are the children's first initials in diamonds. Inside are their birth dates. The egg's surface is studded with diamonds and gold garlands inlaid with rose and ruby flowers, and the surprise inside is a tiny copy of the Alexander Palace, the imperial family's favorite residence. Working in utmost secrecy, highly skilled craftsmen often took more than a year to make each egg.

> " There are people who already have enough diamonds and pearls."
> Peter Carl Fabergé

The first Fabergé egg was crafted by Peter Carl Fabergé for Czar Alexander III to give to his wife in 1885. She was so delighted that Alexander commissioned Fabergé to make her an egg at Easter every year. He was given complete design freedom but with one specification: each egg had to contain a surprise. After Alexander's death in 1894, his son, Nicholas II, continued the egg-giving tradition in 1917. The Moscow Kremlin Egg was inspired by the cathedral in Moscow where the Russian czars were crowned. Made in 1906, it is flanked by four turrets, two with chiming clocks, and a replica of the cathedral's interior inside. The surprise is a gold clockwork music box.

 Russian Nested Doll **from a design by Sergey Malyutin** 1890

i Onyx, four shades of gold, silver, white and green enamel, glass, oil painting.

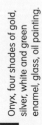
Rose Trellis Egg **Henrik Wigström for Fabergé** 1907

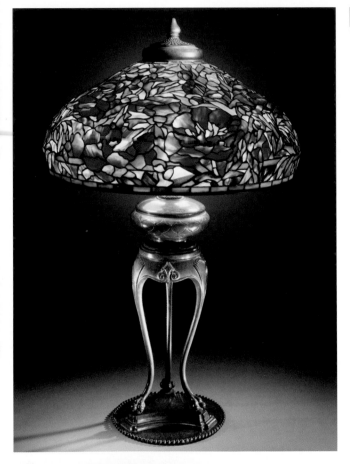

I have always striven to fix beauty in wood, stone, glass, or pottery, in oil or watercolor by using whatever seemed fittest for the expression of beauty; that has been my creed."

Louis Comfort Tiffany

Favrile glass, copper strips, bronze. The mottled and varied colors of Tiffany lamps are a large part of their appeal and distinctiveness.

Peony Tiffany Lamp c.1915
Louis Comfort Tiffany

U.S. artist and designer Louis Comfort Tiffany established Tiffany Glass Company in New York in 1885, producing mosaics, lighting, glassware, jewelry, and stained glass. The firm became particularly well known for its colored glass lampshades, which were influenced by Art Nouveau and the Aesthetic Movement. Featuring stylized, organic decorations, such as flowers, butterflies, and dragonflies, the lampshades were made of pieces of colored glass welded together with strips of copper. Tiffany produced his own opalescent glass in various colors and textures, which had a unique sheen and beauty. His inherent glass-coloring techniques contrasted with the painting on colorless glass that had been the main method of creating stained glass for centuries. In this Peony design, the contrasting red petals and green leaves interlock and appear to overlap as if in nature. From 1894, Tiffany glass became known by the trademarked term "Favrile," which comes from the Old French word for "handmade."

Some of Tiffany's most successful lampshade designs, such as Dragonfly, Peony, and Oriental Poppy (above), were created by Clara Driscoll, who worked in the Tiffany workshop for over twenty years. To create this jewel-bright shade, the petal and leaf shapes were traced onto glass around templates, then cut out individually. Although Tiffany produced many lampshade ranges, each was made by hand. The naturally occurring, subtle variations imbued a unique, hand-crafted quality.

Dragonfly Lamp
Clara Driscoll for Tiffany
c.1900–1906

Wisteria Lamp
Clara Driscoll for Tiffany
c.1901

Jugendstil Table Lamp
Peter Behrens
1902

Les Coprins Lamp
Emile Gallé
1902

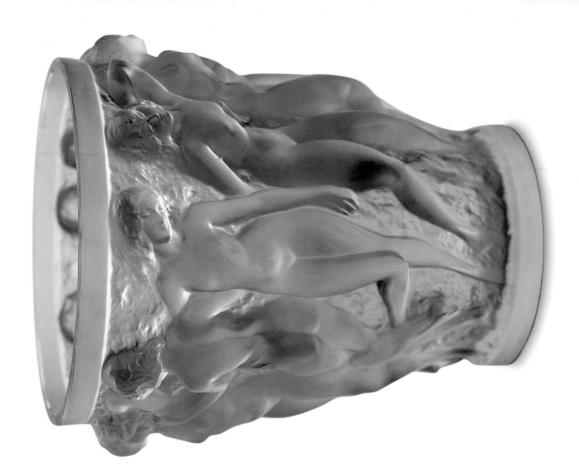

Bacchantes Vase 1927
René Lalique

The rhythmical bas-relief Bacchantes vase was produced in opalescent, smoked, and crystal glass. Lalique worked predominantly with glass made of potash, which had half the lead content of crystal. Called "demi-crystal," it was perfect for the press molding technique he used—molten glass was pressed firmly into steel molds and finished by hand. The small differences that occurred made each piece seem exclusive. Lalique also created glass objects using the "lost wax" process, in which the glass is first modeled in wax and then encased in a plaster mold.

René Lalique revolutionized the production of glass by using new industrial techniques, which made beautiful glassware affordable for ordinary people. Combining his creative talents with foresight and innovation, the designer founded his own firm in Paris in 1885. In 1927, he created this Bacchantes vase, which demonstrates his ability to blend elements of Art Nouveau, Art Deco, and Neoclassicism. The sculptural and curvaceous Bacchantes (priestesses of Bacchus) appear to dance sensuously around the opalescent vase, its soft blue and yellow sheen created by adding metal oxide crystals to the glass mix.

> *I worked tirelessly . . . to achieve a new result and create something that has not yet been seen."*
>
> René Lalique

Peacock Feather Vase
Eugène Feuillâtre
c.1900

Suzanne Statuette
René Lalique
1925

Opalescent glass, frosted and polished. The vase stands 9⅝ inches (24.5 cm) high.

Earthenware, enamel paint, glaze. Crocus was produced on a wide range of china.

Crocus Crockery 1928
Clarice Cliff

From the age of seventeen, Clarice Cliff trained as an apprentice potter. Her versatile creative flair was soon noticed, and in 1927 she was given her own studio at Newport Pottery in the West Midlands, to work as a ceramic artist. From the start, she decorated some of the imperfect white glazed ware in her own dynamic style. Featuring "onglaze" enamel colors, her designs were brighter than most other ceramics available, and she soon produced several ranges under her own label, "Bizarre." They were not only affordable but also admired for their Art Deco–inspired patterns and colors. In 1928, Cliff created a hand-painted pattern of crocuses, each constructed simply and confidently. Initially, only one painter was needed, but as orders poured in, teams of "Crocus girls" were trained, with two or three doing the petals, a "leafer," and a "bander." Cliff also designed the shapes of her pottery, often using geometric forms.

One of Cliff's most popular designs, Crocus was painted with three or four simple downward strokes meeting at the base of the object. This was then turned upside down and thin green lines were painted as leaves. Cliff originally painted Crocus in her favorite vibrant orange, blue, and purple, with a band of yellow above, representing the sun, and one of brown for the earth below. Later, she produced several other color variations, including Purple, Blue, Sungleam, and Spring.

Appliqué Lugano
Clarice Cliff
1930

Colored Earthenware
Charlotte Rhead
c. 1930

Kestrel
Susie Cooper
1932

Honolulu
Clarice Cliff
1933

INDIVIDUALITY

 Beautiful forms and compositions are not made by chance, nor can they ever, in any material, be made at small expense. A composition for cheapness and not excellence of workmanship is the most frequent and certain cause of the rapid decay and entire destruction of arts and manufactures."

Josiah Wedgwood

Jasperware, porcelain. This vase, with its multiple references to the classical world, was made as a gift to the British Museum in London.

Pegasus Vase 1786
Josiah Wedgwood

Named after the winged horse on the lid, this vase closely resembles an ancient Greek amphora, but it was actually modeled in 1786 for Josiah Wedgwood by artist John Flaxman Jr., who integrated several individual, classical ideas. The figures in the main scene are based on an engraving of a Greek vase of the fourth century BCE, showing the Apotheosis of Homer, with Homer accompanied by winged goddesses. The Medusa heads on the handles are taken from an engraving of an antique sandal, and encircling the vase are figures of Apollo and the nine Muses. After the excavations at Pompeii and Herculaneum, and the discoveries of Greek vases in Etruscan tombs, enthusiasm for classical art swept across Europe and the United States. At the same time, Wedgwood developed jasperware, a type of fine matte pottery, which he named after an ancient mineral used to make antique pots and vases.

Wedgwood's jasperware was a dense, hard stoneware that he colored with metallic oxides and decorated with classical ornamentation, usually in contrasting white bas-relief. The first colors of jasperware were blue, amber, and green, but, later, it was also produced in dark blue, sage, olive-green, and lavender with white decoration. The eloquence of the ancient Greek- and Roman-inspired designs was largely thanks to Flaxman, a neoclassical sculptor and designer, who was extremely sympathetic to the concept.

Silver Vase	*Vase du Roi*	*Dancing Hours Bas-Relief*	*Majolica Vase*
Robert Adam	**Sèvres Porcelain**	**John Flaxman for Josiah**	**Josiah Spode**
1770–1771	**Company** c.1776	**Wedgwood** 1776–1778	c.1790–1810

Decanter 1904–1905
Charles Robert Ashbee

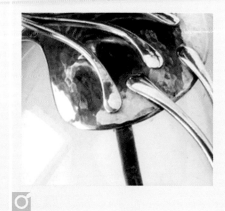

This elegant and sinuous silver handle is attached in a simple and practical way to the delicate green glass decanter. As in all of his designs, Ashbee resisted any artificial illusions, and the gracefully arched silver wires were visibly soldered into place. In 1888, he set up the Guild and School of Handicraft in London, a workshop that adhered to the philosophies of the Arts and Crafts Movement, where craftspeople worked to create individual, high-quality, handmade objects.

Charles Robert Ashbee was an English designer, writer, architect, and social reformer, as well as a leading figure in the Arts and Crafts Movement. When he made this decanter during the early years of the Edwardian period, the Victorian vogue for excessive ornamentation prevailed, but Ashbee's designs were far plainer. He created a wide range of objects with smooth contours, a minimum of materials, and restrained embellishment. Based on an Elizabethan sherry bottle, found during the building of his London house, this decanter followed the dictum of the Arts and Crafts Movement that handmade goods were always superior to mass-produced items.

> [We have] … been engaged in the making of things that we consider the public ought to want, provided meanwhile that the man that makes them is the happier in their making."
> **Charles Robert Ashbee**

Glass, silver, chrysoprase. Ashbee designed different versions of this decanter.

Chalice
Charles Robert Ashbee
1901–1902

Silver and Glass Decanter
Archibald Knox
1903–1904

Lily Pond Window c. 1912
Jacques Gruber

From about 1880 to 1914, Art Nouveau flourished in Europe, particularly in France. Gruber worked alongside all the well-known glass artists of the Ecole de Nancy, and, from 1904, in his own studio in Paris. His delicate and expressive stained glass designs, infused with clear, vivid colorings and sinuous, organic shapes, depicted the natural themes of Art Nouveau with vitality. In his Lily Pond window, for example, contrasting contours, variegated blues, greens, golds, and white, and intricate details, such as layered leaves and petals and soft tonal gradations portraying water, all combined to create a sense of serenity and atmosphere. The design epitomized the optimism of the early twentieth century, before World War I broke out.

Jacques Gruber worked with the Daum brothers and Louis Majorelle in Nancy, France, the center of European glassmaking at the turn of the twentieth century. While creating glass vases for the Nancy designers, he invented a process of laying colored glass over white, and from 1893, when he began producing his own stained glass windows, he adapted his process by etching with hydrofluoric acid. With undulating lines and gem-like colors, he exploited the dynamism of Art Nouveau, and his stained glass designs consolidated his artistic reputation.

The study of nature, the love of nature's art, and the need to express what one feels in one's heart."

Emile Gallé
Art Nouveau designer

 Stained glass, lead came. The natural themes were inspired by fine art and contemporary design.

 Peacock Window
John La Farge
1892–1908

Four Seasons Window
Louis Comfort Tiffany
1900

Rose Window for Hill House
Charles Rennie Mackintosh
1904

> "We should work for simple, good, undecorated things, but things which are in harmony with the human being and organically suited to the little man in the street."

Alvar Aalto

Mold-blown glass. The vase was first made in clear, brown, azure, green, and smoke-colored versions; later, in opal, cobalt, and ruby.

Savoy Vase 1936
Alvar Aalto

The Aalto vase was created by Finnish designer Alvar Aalto and his wife, Aino Marsio. It became known as the Savoy vase because it was part of the furnishings and fixtures created by the couple for the new Savoy restaurant in Helsinki. The design won first prize in a competition in 1936, held by the glass companies Karhula and Iittala, which were looking for a glass object to be displayed in the Finnish Pavilion at the World's Fair in Paris in 1937. Unlike most vases, the Savoy vase is asymmetrical, its upright shape forming a series of individually sized undulations. The design is said to be inspired by Aalto's drawing of the dress of a Sami woman, which depicts her leather breeches. The designer's prototypes for the vase were made by blowing glass into an arrangement of wooden sticks stuck into the ground, and letting the molten glass swell on some of the sides but not others. This process created the iconic wavy outline.

The fluency of the shape of the Savoy vase reminded many of the landscape of Finland. Aalto was determined to explore organic themes, and the vase closely matched his early drawings, showing different sized curves and waves. Where the glass bends, it appears either darker and denser or lighter and more transparent, which makes it aesthetically appealing whether or not it contains flowers. After initial technical problems in making the vase with molds of thin steel creating the shape, it was produced in a variety of colors and sizes.

Jack-in-the-Pulpit Vase **Louis Comfort Tiffany and Thomas Manderson** 1900–1912

Blue Melusin **Loetz** 1905

Steuben Aurene Vase **Steuben Glassworks** c. 1915

Glass Pitcher **Aino Marsio** 1932

Stainless steel. Every item of Wright's flatware was stamped from one sheet of stainless steel.

In the middle of the twentieth century, Russel Wright created household products that reflected the growing desire for relaxed, informal living that existed after World War II. Comfort and convenience were eclipsing the focus on decoration and embellishment of the previous decades, and Wright's individual and practical housewares emphasized his belief that the dining table was the center of the home. Determining to bring modern, affordable design to the general public, he produced his line of American Modern dinnerware in 1937, which was a huge commercial success. To complement it, he created affordable, ergonomic flatware, characterized by minimal, elegant forms with smooth contours and long handles that contrasted with the abbreviated fork prongs. Each piece of Wright's American Modern flatware was plain, devoid of applied ornamentation, and harmoniously balanced.

Through his ergonomically designed American Modern flatware and dinnerware (above)—it was the most widely sold tableware in U.S. history—Wright enticed ordinary Americans to embrace modernism. His simple designs created a significant impact in homes across the United States and beyond. Wright also wrote, with his wife, a best-selling book, *Guide to Easier Living* (1950), which explained how to reduce housework and increase leisure time through efficient design and management.

Ingram Street Tea Room Flatware **Charles Rennie Mackintosh** 1900–1912

Pride Flatware **David Mellor** 1953

Campden Flatware **Robert Welch for Oneida** 1955

Concorde Flatware **Raymond Loewy for Air France** c.1978

 Although Arne Jacobsen insisted that he was an architect and not a designer, he produced some of the most iconic chairs of the twentieth century. Amalgamating Scandinavian and modernist design, he created the Model 3100, which soon became known as the Ant chair, in collaboration with his team of designers, which included Verner Panton. Light, stable, and stackable, it was nicknamed the "Ant" chair after its individual shape, which resembled the silhouette of an ant with a raised head. Originally designed to be used in the canteen of the Danish pharmaceutical company Novo Nordisk, it was the first mass-produced chair to have a seat and back formed from one piece of wood.

Molded, laminated plywood, lacquer, steel. Pictured is Model 3107, also made in 1952. Its flat top contrasts with the curved Model 3100.

Ant Chair 1952
Arne Jacobsen

"I do not feel certain until I have confronted my initial solution with other solutions—although in fact the first solution often proves to be the right one."
Arne Jacobsen

The original version of Jacobsen's minimalist Ant chair had three plastic legs and a seat made from laminated veneer. It inspired him to make a series of chairs in slightly varied shapes, using different materials, but all with one piece forming the seat and back (left). Influenced by other contemporary designs that used molded plywood, Jacobsen worked out a new technique of bending plywood in three dimensions. In 1963, after a scandalous affair with British government minister John Profumo, Christine Keeler posed naked on a copy of one of these chairs in a photograph by Lewis Morley. The Ant chair became an icon of its time.

Molded Plywood Chair
Charles and Ray Eames
1946

Pretzel Chair
George Nelson
1952

Tulip Armchair
Eero Saarinen
1955–1956

Swan Chair
Arne Jacobsen
1958

Eames Lounge Chair and Ottoman 1956
Charles and Ray Eames

Although the Eames lounge chair and ottoman were initially made with five thin layers of wood veneer, they are currently made with seven layers of rosewood veneer. From the start, the emphasis was on comfort, with three plywood shells forming the seat and back and one forming the ottoman. Charles and Ray Eames were two of the most important post–World War II designers, and when they produced this undulating furniture, they had been exploring ways of using interlocking pieces of molded plywood in furniture for almost a decade. The spaces between the seat and back give support without restriction, while a joint and washer at the back creates flexibility, allowing the sitter to gently recline or rock.

Originally designed as a present for filmmaker Billy Wilder, a friend of Charles and Ray Eames, this chair and ottoman were the result of the U.S. designers' early attempts to bend plywood using heat pressure in 1940. After years of development, the chair was produced commercially in 1956. Charles said he had aimed to make a chair with "the warm, receptive look of a well-used first baseman's mitt." With its generous proportions and integral plump leather cushions, the chair molds individually to accommodate any sitter.

Eventually everything connects—people, ideas, objects. The quality of the connections is the key to quality per se."
Charles Eames

Laminated rosewood veneer, leather, aluminum. The Eames chair was made for comfort.

Molded Plywood Chair
Charles and Ray Eames
1946

La Chaise
Charles and Ray Eames
1948

Wire Mesh Chair
Charles and Ray Eames
1951–1953

Bookworm Shelf 1993–1995
Ron Arad

At the end of the twentieth century, there was a surge in the development of inexpensive, functional synthetic materials and several designers made use of them. Arad's utilitarian Bookworm bookshelf, made of a long, thin, flat piece of plastic with movable brackets, is an example. Affordable and adjustable, with eleven small box-like brackets, which can be screwed on either side, the shelf can be configured to fit into particular spaces or to create a certain look.

This witty, meandering bookshelf, created by provocative Israeli architect and designer Ron Arad, was unveiled initially in 1993 at the Milan Furniture Fair. Although designed as an individual item made of sprung steel, it was soon mass-produced by Italian manufacturer Kartell in injection-molded PVC, and it has since become one of Arad's best-selling works. Rebelling against conventional shelving and exploiting the paradox of steel in an organic form. Arad created a bookshelf that could be adapted by the user to create individual arrangements. By changing the position of the brackets, the shelf can be manipulated into numerous curvilinear shapes when hung on a wall.

> *I can't claim I design to save or improve the world. . . . Luckily, what I do is useful for other people."*
> **Ron Arad**

Batch-dyed, injection-molded PVC. The Bookworm is the antithesis of traditional shelves.

Narrow Pappardelle Chair **Ron Arad** 1992–1998

Lovely Rita Bookshelf **Ron Arad for Kartell** 1995

FORM

Le Parfait Jars c. 1825
Unknown

With their distinctive orange rubber seals and clip-tops, Le Parfait jars are extremely effective in conserving all kinds of food and drink. Le Parfait was established in the early 1930s, in Reims, France, and manufactured the jars in many sizes, expressly to store food simply and naturally without losing any flavor. The combination of the rubber ring and metal bail sealing system preserves the contents for a lengthy period, while the wire clip easily opens the jars, releasing the vacuum.

Until the early nineteenth century, food preservation processes, such as salting, smoking, and pickling, were time-consuming and altered the flavors and quality of the treated food. Then, in 1810, Nicolas Appert, a French chef and distiller, discovered that enclosing food in airtight containers preserved it for longer than any other known method. Based on this, in about 1825, a designer, whose name has been lost, produced jars made of sturdy pressed glass with flip-top lids that were sealed with rubber rings and that, when shut, formed a vacuum. The wide-necked jars with their unique sealing lids have hardly changed in design since their conception.

Perfection is finally attained not when there is no longer anything to add, but when there is no longer anything to take away."

Antoine de Saint-Exupéry
writer

Pressed glass, rubber, aluminum. Despite its patents, the design has been imitated repeatedly.

Kilner Jar
John Kilner
c. 1842

Mason Jar
John Landis Mason
1858

Tupperware
Earl S. Tupper
1946

Bentwood Chair 1859
Michael Thonet

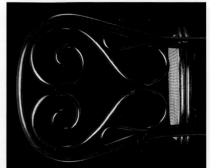

Using as few parts as possible, Thonet aimed to manufacture many different models of the bentwood chair. Each one was cost-effective, gracefully curved, and comfortable. Chair No. 4 (left), with its decorative S-shaped design on the backrest, was made between 1881 and 1890. Thonet's company, Gebrüder Thonet, published catalogs, numbered every chair model, and exhibited at international fairs rapidly gaining a worldwide reputation. A unique system aided Thonet's success: all the chairs were delivered in pieces and assembled at their destination.

Originally designed in 1859, the No. 14 is thought to be the first mass-produced chair. In 1842, Michael Thonet was awarded a patent for a process he had invented that enabled him to bend laminated and sold beechwood easily and cheaply using steam and pressure. Until then, most chairs had been made by hand, but Thonet's method allowed him to manufacture large quantities of lightweight, durable chairs. Early versions of the No. 14 chair were glued together, but, by 1861, screws were used instead. From 1867, it was made from just six parts, ten screws, and two washers. By 1930, about fifty million No. 14 chairs had been sold.

There is absolutely nothing more elegant, superior in concept, more precise in its construction, or more practical."

Le Corbusier
architect

Rocking Chair No. 1
Michael Thonet
1860

Beechwood, cane, metal. The No. 14 was the prototype for mass-produced furniture.

Sitting Machine
Josef Hoffmann
c. 1905

Our chairs, tables, and closets, as well as other appropriated objects, are the 'abstract-real' sculptures of our future interiors."

Theo van Doesburg
artist

Painted and lacquered beech and plywood, *c.*1923. The chair is designed to keep the sitter upright and awake.

Red and Blue Chair 1918
Gerrit Rietveld

Searching for a universal form of expression with this chair, Gerrit Rietveld adhered to the principles of the art movement De Stijl (also known as neoplasticism). Trained as both a cabinetmaker and an architect, he formed a prototype for this chair in unlacquered, unpainted beechwood in 1918. With cheap machine production in mind, the frame was made from several standard lengths of beechwood and thin pine planks, with two boards forming the seat and backrest. Rietveld officially joined De Stijl in 1919. In about 1923, he painted the chair black with blocks of primary colors to accentuate its spatial boundaries and to correspond with the movement's ideals. De Stijl members also advocated that design should appeal to the viewer spiritually. With its angled, defined planes, Rietveld's chair was an abstract construction, with neither volume nor mass, and an item of furniture that did not seem to enclose space.

Rietveld's chair references paintings by the De Stijl artists Piet Mondrian and Theo van Doesburg, for example, *Contra-Composition of Dissonances, XVI* (1925) by van Doesburg (above). A work of art as well as a practical object, the chair recalls De Stijl's aesthetic philosophies and could also be mass-produced. Along with Mondrian and van Doesburg, Rietveld employed lines and planes to create boundaries, and used a restricted palette of red, blue, yellow, black, white, and gray.

Cabaret Fledermaus Chair	*Transat Chair*	*Steltman Chair*	*Dry Chair*
Josef Hoffmann	**Eileen Gray**	**Gerrit Rietveld**	**Massimo Morozzi**
c.1905–1906	1925–1930	1963	1987

Chanel No.5 Perfume Bottle 1921
Gabrielle "Coco" Chanel

The Chanel No. 5 bottle was deliberately angular and understated. Machine-made and mass-produced, it embraced modernism in all aspects, even the black sans serif text of the label. Following Chanel's own motto: "Always remove, always strip away, never add," the design has remained more or less the same. The first bottle, sold only to select clients, had small, slightly rounded shoulders. In 1924, when Parfums Chanel was established, it was adjusted slightly and given geometrically faceted corners to reflect contemporary Art Deco tastes.

In 1921, Gabrielle "Coco" Chanel launched her signature perfume, No. 5. The first fashion designer to produce a synthetic perfume, rather than the traditional floral compounds, she also designed a bottle that contrasted with contemporary ornate and feminine designs. The plain, rectangular form was probably inspired by the beveled Charvet toiletry flacons and the whiskey decanter used by her lover, Arthur "Boy" Capel, as well as glass pharmaceutical vials. The bottle retains its modern aura despite changing fashions. The octagonal stopper, created in 1924, recalls the shape of Place Vendôme, Paris, the location of Hôtel Ritz, where Chanel lived intermittently from 1920.

" In order to be
irreplaceable one
*must always be
different."*

Gabrielle "Coco"
Chanel

Glass, paper, ink. In its elegant bottle, No. 5 remains the world's top-selling perfume.

Guerlain Djedi Flacon
Georges Chevalier
1926

Le Baiser du Faune
René Lalique
c.1923

Skyscraper Furniture c. 1927
Paul T. Frankl

Imitating the new soaring skyscrapers of U.S. cities, particularly New York (left), Frankl's stacked structures were instantly recognizable and appealed to the public, rich and poor alike. Frankl employed his architectural skills to create towering vertical lines that were counterbalanced by stable, horizontal planes. Conveying the feeling of freedom felt by many after World War I and shedding retrospective design styles, the designs helped to shape American modernism.

Paul T. Frankl trained as an architect in Berlin and moved to the United States in his late twenties. Enthralled by the sense of excitement in New York, he settled there and created a bookcase for his personal use based on the jagged Manhattan skyline. When neighbors admired it, he designed more items of furniture, all formed following the shapes of the skyscrapers around him. Eventually he opened a showroom, where he sold his unique Art Deco and modernist-inspired designs. With boxy lower sections and elongated upper parts, his skyscraper furniture reflected the sense of abandonment of the past, confidence in the present, and hope for the future felt by many, particularly in the United States, before the Depression and World War II.

" Our progress . . . does not depend or fighting for modernism, but on educating ourselves to be part of the world we live in."

Paul T. Frankl

Maple, Bakelite. Skyscraper furniture brought a fresh perspective to U.S. design.

+ Skyscrape Bookcase and Desk
Paul T. Frankl c. 1928

Wiener Bookcase
Émile-Jacques Ruhlmann
1929

> *We should work for simple, good, undecorated things, but things which are in harmony with the human being and organically suited to the little man in the street."*

Alvar Aalto

Bent laminated plywood. Aalto made his stools with either three or four legs. Also known as Model No. 60.

L-legged Stacking Stool 1932–1933
Alvar Aalto

Sometimes called the father of Scandinavian modernism, Finnish architect Alvar Aalto focused on functionality, closely followed by comfort. Although he was inspired by modernism, he also believed that good design should be organic, and so he used wood for his furniture, instead of tubular steel, which was quite radical at the time. After much experimentation, he invented new methods for bonding veneers and molding ply, and he attained several patents for bent plywood. In 1932, he formed his L-legged stacking stools of molded plywood, which overcame the common problem of joining legs to main furniture components.

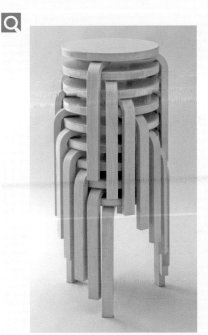

Aalto's innovation of attaching legs directly to the seat of his stacking stools without the need for any additional support was achieved by inserting glued pieces of veneer into vertical slots that had been cut into a straight section of wood. The weakened wood was bent while the glue set, leaving a permanently fixed right angle, which Aalto called the "bent knee." Compact, practical, and orderly, at least sixteen stools can be stacked at a time. Within fifty years of their invention, more than a million stacking stools were in existence. They became the most widely sold item of Aalto's furniture.

Paimio Chair	Folding Chair	Y (or Wishbone) Chair	NXT Stacking Chair
Alvar Aalto	**Mogens Koch**	**Hans J. Wegner**	**Peter Karpf**
1931–1932	1932	1949	1991

Polyurethane foam, colored lacquer. By 1999, polypropylene was used and in a wider range of colors.

S Chair 1959–1960
Verner Panton

This first no-leg, cantilevered, injection-molded chair, formed from a single piece of plastic, symbolizes the optimism, color, and reduced lines of the 1960s. Sleek and shiny, it became known as the S chair after its shape, which was inspired by a stack of buckets. It is also often called the Stacking chair or the Panton chair, after its designer, Verner Panton, who originally trained as an architect. Panton first attempted to create a plastic cantilevered chair in the 1950s, and from 1950 to 1952, he worked for fellow Dane Arne Jacobsen. The two men collaborated on numerous furniture designs, and Jacobsen's intense research into new materials and technologies influenced Panton enormously. Captivated by the potential of plastic, a novel material at the time, Panton determined to create a comfortable chair, made of one piece, that could be used anywhere. The S chair was the result of his extensive experiments.

Seeking the perfect mix of smooth contours, flexibility, durability, and lightness, Panton made the original chair from fiberglass-reinforced polyester, cast in a mold, which was then polished, primed, and painted. Although the chair was conceived in the 1950s, its mass production only became possible in 1967, in collaboration with Vitra, when industrially produced plastics were used. This development led to a marked reduction in costs.

Mezzadro Stool
Achille and Pier Giacomo Castiglioni 1957

Polyprop Chair
Robin Day 1962–1963

Universale Chair
Joe Colombo 1965–1967

Donna Up5 Chair
Gaetano Pesce 1969

iPhone 2007
Jonathan Ive

Innovatively, the entire face of the iPhone is interactive. With its glass screen, chrome-plated metal frame, and instantly recognizable and user-friendly icons, the iPhone, which is larger than most other cell phones, invites interaction. Ive explained that his obsessive attention to detail meant that he considered aspects often overlooked by others, and he mirrored the philosophies of designer Dieter Rams in focusing on users' needs rather than on the device itself. He rebuilt the system with a different design in 2013, when the operating software iOS 7 (left) was introduced.

In the 1980s, Steve Jobs, Apple's co-founder, predicted that cell phones would become as important as personal computers. In 2007, he linked the two and launched the iPhone. With persistent experiments into the use of new tools, materials, and production processes, Apple's chief designer, Jonathan Ive, created an accessible and ergonomic form to accommodate the pioneering touch-screen technology. By either tapping or sliding the screen, users can connect with the phone immediately and intuitively. Within a year of its launch, the iPhone was named "Invention of the Year" by *Time* magazine. By the end of 2008, more than six million iPhones had been sold.

I'm constantly haunted by thoughts of, is it good enough? Is there any way we could have made it better?"

Jonathan Ive

The original iPhone was made of chrome, glass, aluminum, and plastic.

iMac
Jonathan Ive
1998

iPod
Jonathan Ive
2001

BlackBerry 10
Todd Wood
2013

FUNCTION

Automatic Tape Measure 1842
James Chesterman

Ever inventive, Chesterman patented a special heating technique for flat wire in 1853. Flat wire was generally used to structure wide crinoline skirts, and Chesterman's innovative process made the wire particularly strong and relatively easy to produce in continuous lengths. Nevertheless, when crinolines became unfashionable, sales of Chesterman's flat wire diminished. Consequently, he decided to use the product for his automatic tape measure; the flat wire ensured that the tape was resilient and lightweight and that its reach could be extensive. A brass handle on top of the circular case coiled the measuring tape inside and folded flat when the device was not in use.

In 1821, James Chesterman of Chesterman Steel Company in England was granted a patent for his innovative automatic method of rewinding a tape measure using a spring mechanism. It was not until 1842, however, that he designed his pocket measuring tape. Initially, the tape, made from woven cloth reinforced with wire strands, was considered too flimsy. Later, by using his method of heating and riveting long strips of fine steel, Chesterman created a pliable tape that could be wound inside a small, round leather case. When pulled out, the fine, steel tape remained straight and flat, which was far more practical and functional than his earlier design.

[The steel tape] is about the most unique thing of the kind we have ever seen."

Scientific American magazine

Automatic tape measure, late nineteenth century, made of leather, steel, and brass.

Spring Measuring Tape
Alvin J. Fellows
1868

Farrand Rapid Rule
Hiram Farrand and the Brown Company 1922

DISTO™ Laser Measure
Leica
1993

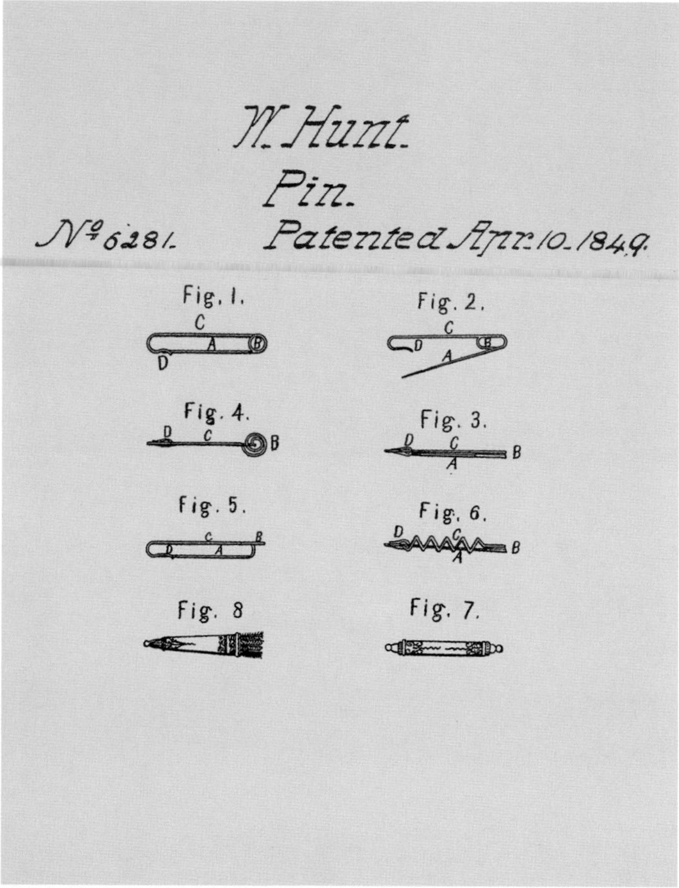

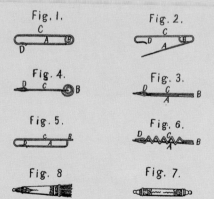

W. Hunt.

Pin.

N⁰ 6281. Patented Apr. 10. 1849.

Fig. 1.

Fig. 2.

Fig. 4.

Fig. 3.

Fig. 5.

Fig. 6.

Fig. 8.

Fig. 7.

While wondering how to settle a fifteen-dollar debt to a friend, Walter Hunt, a mechanic from New York, sat fiddling with a piece of brass wire. Eventually, he coiled the wire into an oval, with a spring at one end and a clasp at the other. The point of the wire could be pushed into the clasp by the spring, where it would remain, protecting the user from injury. When pressed slightly, the spring opened the pin with a simple movement. In one evening, Hunt created a prototype and several design sketches. By April 1849, he had acquired a patent for his safety pin, which he sold to W. R. Grace and Company for four hundred dollars. He repaid his debt, and kept the remaining money for himself, while W. R. Grace and Company went on to make millions of dollars from his invention. The design of the safety pin has remained virtually the same ever since. Although a prolific inventor, Hunt received little recognition in his lifetime.

Steel or brass. Walter Hunt's original drawings of his safety pin; the design was patented in 1849.

Safety Pin 1849
Walter Hunt

For me the safety pin is about rebellion, and I'm punk in the soul ... I was always pushing for something that nobody did."
Donatella Versace
fashion designer

The safety pin has become an essential item for billions of people all over the world, with innumerable uses. Hunt realized the practicality of his invention, but probably not how indispensable it would become. In the late 1970s, safety pins also became used as fashion statements, incorporated into clothing and body piercings as part of the early rebelliousness connected with the punk movement. Later, as punk was adopted by fashion designers, safety pins became crucial components of many chain store and couture clothes. Models and celebrities were snapped wearing provocative garments, seemingly held together by oversized safety pins. Christy Turlington models such a dress (left) for Versace's fall/winter 1992/93 collection.

Paper Clip
Johan Vaaler/William Middlebrook 1899

Pushpin
Edwin Moore
1900

Bobby Pin/Hair Grip
Unknown designer
c.1910

Phillips Head Screw
Henry F. Phillips
c.1932

75

A. W. FABER

Faber-Castell Colored Pencils 1856

Lothar von Faber

German cabinetmaker Kaspar Faber began making graphite pencils in 1761. In 1839, his great-grandson, Lothar von Faber, took over the business and, through various entrepreneurial strategies, expanded it to become a worldwide company. Focusing on quality and function, and paying great attention to detail, he modernized production methods. Lothar used better materials, built factories, opened new stores, branded his pencils, and increased the number of products. This included the development of a range of colored pencils, made with a combination of pigments and a clay and wax binder. In 1898, as a result of marriage, "Castell" was added to the company name.

Constantly aware of competitors, Faber continued to improve the production and quality of its colored pencils. By 1904, modifications had been made to their texture and vibrancy and, by 1924, more than sixty different colors were being produced. As the twentieth century progressed, Faber-Castell created even more colors and new ranges. In 2001, it began manufacturing triangular-shaped pencils (left) to give the user a firmer grip when writing and drawing.

> *From the beginning I strove to rise to the highest position by producing the best that could be made in the whole world."*
>
> **Lothar von Faber**

Cedarwood, pigments, clay and wax binder. This pencil set was marketed in 1908.

Colored Oil Pastel Pencil
Johann Sebastian Staedtler 1834

No. 19 Range
Derwent
1930s

Steel, hardwood. Most Swiss army knives have small indentations for extracting the tools with a thumbnail.

Swiss Army Knife 1891
Karl Elsener

This foldaway miniature toolkit was designed by trained cutler Karl Elsener, expressly for the Swiss army. Intended for soldiers, specifically to open canned food and to dismantle rifles, Elsener's original knife included a blade, reamer (hole piercer), can opener, and screwdriver, which all folded into the handle of the knife. Yet this first knife was not well received, and, by 1896, Elsener had redesigned it, this time attaching tools on both sides of the handle using an innovative spring mechanism. The following year, his more functional new knife, featuring the same implements as the first, plus a second smaller blade, a corkscrew, and wood fiber grips, was welcomed by the army and by the public, too. Elsener named his expanding company after his mother, Victoria, and, in 1921, combined her name with the shortened international name for stainless steel, "inox" (from the French *acier inoxydable*), to make "Victorinox."

Once Elsener had designed his second knife, demand increased and variations proliferated. Today, the two allied companies of Victorinox and Wenger produce many different models, such as the ToolChest Plus (above). With multiple functions and uses, these knives are recognized for their supreme versatility and reliability. Now made of stainless steel and plastic, they include tools such as tweezers, pliers, bottle openers, magnifying glasses, and scissors.

| *Swiss Officer's Knife* **Karl Elsener** 1897 | *Pocket Survival Tool* **Tim Leatherman** 1984 | *Wenger SwissGrip* **Wenger** 1996 | *Victorinox Tomo* **Kazuma Yamaguchi** 2011 |

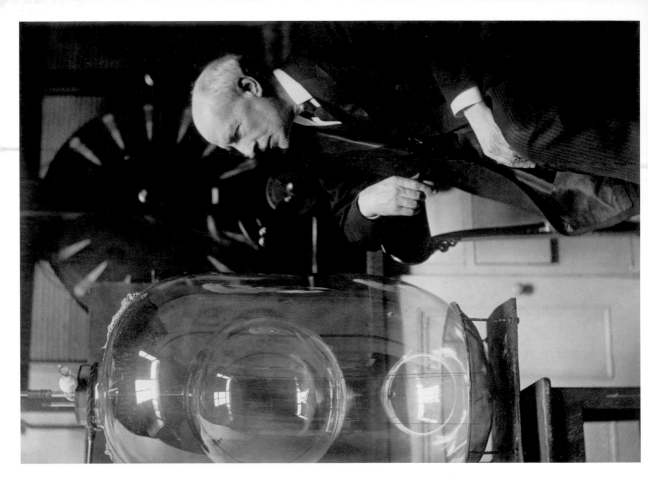

Vacuum Flask 1892
James Dewar

Within twelve years of Dewar inventing the vacuum flask (left), many different forms were designed and produced for both domestic and industrial use. All were based on Dewar's discovery that most heat entering or escaping any vessel does so through the neck or lid, while a near-vacuum in the space between the two flasks prevents this. The original Dewar flask was made of glass, while commercial vacuum flasks are made of various materials. A typical domestic flask can keep liquids warm for eight hours or cool for twenty-four.

The vacuum flask, also known as a Dewar flask, Dewar bottle, or Thermos, keeps its contents, which are usually liquid, hot or cold for several hours, irrespective of the surrounding temperature. Invented by Sir James Dewar in 1892, especially to store chemicals at constant temperatures for scientific experiments, it consists of two flasks, one within the other, joined at the neck. It functions by air being partially evacuated between the inner and outer flasks, creating a near-vacuum, which prevents heat transfer. Dewar did not patent his invention, and, in 1904, a German glass technician realized its potential as a commercial item and trademarked it under the name Thermos, from the Greek word *therme*, meaning "heat."

*Minds are
like parachutes,
they only
function when
they are open."*
James Dewar

Thermos Flask
Reinhold Burger
1904

James Dewar, c.1910,
with a vacuum flask of
brass and glass.

Thermos Flask
Sanders, Frary & Clark
1914

> "Dualit toasters are hand-built and our lads have pride in their work. They're designed for longevity . . . the looks are a bonus."

Leslie Gort-Barten
managing director, Dualit

Cast aluminum. Made and patented in 1946, this was the first flip-sided toaster with the unique "stay-warm" promise.

Dualit Toaster 1946
Max Gort-Barten

After settling in Britain, Swiss-German engineer Max Gort-Barten began manufacturing household products. His first was the Dual-Light Fire, a two-bar electric heater that was also a light. Following on from the Dual-Light's success, he used the name "Dualit" for his next product: a small electric toaster for the domestic market. In order to survive increasing competition in the consumer market, he created a toaster for the catering trade in 1952, which was the first in the world to function with an integral timer. Additionally, the toast did not pop up when it was ready, as was usual with most other toasters; it remained inside, keeping warm until the user pressed the eject lever. Gort-Barton designed his toasters specifically to withstand the demands of commercial kitchens, but, since the 1980s, they have also been greatly coveted for domestic use. Combining a streamlined appearance with functionality and reliability, Dualit toasters featured a unique mechanism that enabled bread to be toasted on both sides at the same time.

Although the design of Dualit toasters has evolved over the years, their original smooth and shiny appearance (above) has been retained, and the user still has complete control. By the late 1940s, all Dualit toasters were made from stainless steel and cast aluminum, which ensured that the toast remained fresh and hot. The Dualit toaster became a must-have kitchen appliance in the 1980s and it is now available in a range of colors.

Model D-12 Toaster	*Automatic Pop-up Toaster*	*Star Toaster*	*Sunbeam Model T-9*
General Electric	**Charles P. Strite**	**Maniby Fitzgerald**	**George Scharfenberg**
1909	1921	1922	1939

Stainless steel, glass, canvas,
polysulfone. This Polaroid Land Camera
Model 95A dates from 1954.

Polaroid Land Camera Model 95 1948
Edwin H. Land

Inspired by his young daughter's question about why photographs did not appear immediately from a camera once they were taken, U.S. scientist Edwin Land founded the Polaroid Corporation in 1937 and pioneered instant photography. He claimed that, within an hour of considering the problem, he had worked out the physical chemistry and how to make a camera and a film that produced instant photographs. In 1948, he began selling the Polaroid Land Camera Model 95, which produced positive prints in approximately one minute. The first Polaroids used instant film, which came in two rolls: positive and negative. After 1963, Polaroids used "pack film," which users had to pull out of the camera for development. Once the photograph had developed, the positive image was peeled apart from the negative. Land's original concept was to create a photographic system that was easy to use, and it caught on with the public immediately. The first Polaroids produced only black-and-white images; color was introduced in 1963.

The folding bellows design of the Land Camera was large enough to contain a film pack, and the print was removed from a flap at the back. The first boxy, concertina-like designs relied on diffusion transfer, which moved dyes from the negative image to the positive through a reagent that combined a developer and a fixer. Professional photographers, including Ansel Adams, Pop artist Andy Warhol, and Surrealist photographer Man Ray (above), experimented with the camera.

Highlander Land Camera Model 80A **Polaroid Corporation** 1957–1959	*Swinger Land Camera Model 20* **Polaroid Corporation** 1965–1970	*Digital Camera* **Steven Sasson for Kodak** 1975	*Mavica Analog Camera* **Sony** 1981

The first Swatch watches were true to Hayek's idea of being mass-produced, reliable Swiss timepieces, made of plastic, with a radically reduced number of parts. Swatch has since continued to introduce millions of low-priced watches in different materials, including plastic, stainless steel, aluminum, rubber, and silicone. Various artists and designers have designed Swatches, some in limited editions. They are created for people of all ages, for every occasion, and in a wide assortment of exclusive designs. For example, the Random Ghost Swatch (left) is completely transparent with cut-away dials revealing components in a range of colors, all assembled randomly to make each watch unique.

Swiss watches are acclaimed for their quality craftsmanship and accuracy. In the late 1970s, the watch market suddenly became flooded with cheap quartz watches from Asia, and the Swiss market share dropped from more than 50 percent to just 15. In the early 1980s, entrepreneur Nicolas G. Hayek, had the idea to manufacture inexpensive timepieces with Swiss efficiency and precision; he co-founded Swatch in 1983. Hayek wanted people to own a "second watch" that was not only a superior Swiss watch, with fewer parts than traditional timepieces, but also fun, reliable, and inexpensive.

Keeping dreams alive and trying to make them come true is crucial in the watch business."
Nicolas G. Hayek

Swiss mechanism, various materials. Many styles of Swatch have been made since 1983.

G-Shock DW5000
Kikuo Ibe for Casio
1983

Serpent GZ102 Swatch
Keith Haring
1985

Indiglo Ironman Triathlon
Timex
1992

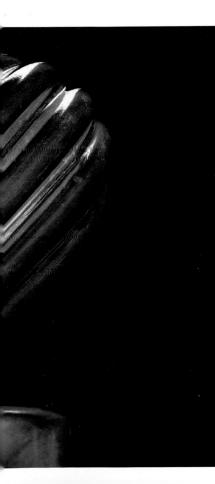

EXPRESSION

> *The world of reality has its limits; the world of imagination is boundless."*

Jean-Jacques Rousseau
philosopher

Oak, pine, Japanese black and gold lacquer, veneer, gilt-bronze, marble.

Console Table c. 1755–1760
Bernard van Risenburgh II

Exploiting the ornamentation and opulence of eighteenth-century Rococo style, Bernard van Risenburgh II created elegant and delicate pieces of furniture that expressed the grandeur of the Louis XV period. This ornate console table with curling scrolls and leaf shapes, decorated in a Japanese style and using the Japanese technique of lacquerwork, is an example of his flamboyance. In contrast to other contemporary furniture, which was usually simply painted, van Risenburgh's designs were enhanced by inlaid porcelain, marquetry, and gilding. The designer stamped all his furniture with his initials: B.V.R.B.

Van Risenburgh first supplied his Japanese lacquer furniture to the French queen consort, Marie Leszczyńska, in 1737. Within a short time, his customers also included the king, Louis XV, the king's mistress, Madame de Pompadour, and other members of the aristocracy. The designer was celebrated for his elegant, embellished furniture, including tables, cupboards, bookcases, and chests of drawers, which featured elaborate floral veneers, Sèvres porcelain plaques, gilding, serpentine cornices, and cabriole legs. Van Risenburgh is considered by many to be the greatest cabinetmaker of Louis XV's reign.

Writing Table
Bernard van Risenburgh II
c. 1755

Mechanical Table
Jean-François Oeben
c. 1761–1763

Jewel Cabinet
William Vile
1762

Roll-top Desk
Jean-Henri Riesener
1769

In 1917, the Massachusetts-based Converse Rubber Shoe Company produced its first basketball sneaker and named it the All Star. Intended for professional basketball players, it comprised a rubber sole and a canvas upper. In 1921, Charles H. "Chuck" Taylor joined the Converse All Stars team, sponsored by the Converse Company. Taylor promoted the All Star sneakers while teaching his sport throughout the United States. He also improved the footwear, enhancing its flexibility, strength, and support. The protective ankle patches displayed the name of the sneakers, giving expression to the design.

In 1923, in recognition of Taylor's work, the Converse Company added his signature to the ankle patch, and the sneakers were referred to as "Converses," "Chucks," or "Chuck Taylors." All Stars soon became popular among professional players in the United States, and were also worn by Olympic athletes, and later, during World War II, by soldiers in training. After the war, All Stars became the sneakers of choice for 90 percent of basketball players. Kentucky teammates Bobby Watson (far left) and Bill Spivey (left) display theirs during a practice session at Madison Square Garden in December 1949.

Canvas, rubber, laces, eyelets. All Stars were the first mass-produced basketball sneakers.

Onitsuka Tiger Corsair
Phil Knight and Bill Bowerman 1969

Air Jordan I
Peter Moore for Nike 1985

Nike Air Max
Nike 1987

Glass Tea Service 1930–1934
Wilhelm Wagenfeld

Wagenfeld developed his tea service to be strong and delicate, simple and elegant, practical and stylish. He was commissioned by Erich Schott, director of Jenaer Glaswerk in Zweisel, Germany, to create useful, appealing, and heat-resistant products. Closely adhering to Bauhaus principles of making designs both utilitarian and aesthetically pleasing, Wagenfeld produced the teapot (left) in three different sizes, with a central diffuser to strain the tea leaves. At first sight, the transparent tea service definitively expresses both its form and function.

Although Wilhelm Wagenfeld designed electrical products for German manufacturer Braun during the 1950s, he is best known for his earlier designs for glassware and ceramics. After studying and teaching at the Bauhaus, he went on to express the principles of clarity and functionalism in his own designs. This tea service typified Wagenfeld's belief in designing objects that were suitable for mass production and that pioneered the use of new materials, too. Made of the same heat-resistant glass that formed test tubes, the glassware was intended for both casual and formal occasions. Although the design is particularly economical, Wagenfeld's individual expression is evident.

The displays in the shop windows of our cities are overflowing with . . . meaningless junk . . . wares have got louder, brasher, more intricate, but not better."
Wilhelm Wagenfeld

Borosilicate glass. The apparent fragility of the design belies its durability and practicality.

Silver Tea Service
Jean Puiforcat
1928

Drop Tea Service
Luigi Colani
1971

Moon Tea Service
Jasper Morrison
1997

Lego® 1958
Ole Kirk and Godtfred Kirk Christiansen

The bright colors, sturdiness, and easy-clean nature of Lego made the design an instant success with parents and children alike. The blocks' simplicity allows children to be creative with them, and their compatibility means that Legos of all kinds, from plain-colored blocks to themed sets, can be used together. Legolands have been built in many locations, featuring themed rides and replicas of several European towns, made entirely from Legos. Educators describe Legos as "socializing and communication-enhancing," and an aid to "perception and comprehension."

During the global depression of the 1930s, Danish cabinetmaker Ole Kirk Christiansen made wooden toys for the children of local farmers. In 1934, he named his small company Lego, a composite of the Danish words *leg* (play) and *godt* (well). After buying the first injection-molding machine in Denmark in 1947, he began casting colorful and durable plastic bricks with small notches and dents—the notch idea came from Ole's son, Godtfred—that enabled them to click together. By 1958, the bricks had been refined into an interlocking Lego system that allowed children to express their individuality. Ten years later, the first Legoland—a theme park made of Lego bricks—was built in Billund.

> The most important function of education at any level is to develop the personality of the individual."
>
> **Ole Kirk Christiansen**

ABS and PC plastics. The first Legoland features a model of Nyhavn waterfront, Copenhagen.

Meccano
Frank Hornby
1898

Fischertechnik
Artur Fischer
1965

K'Nex
Joel Glickman
1993

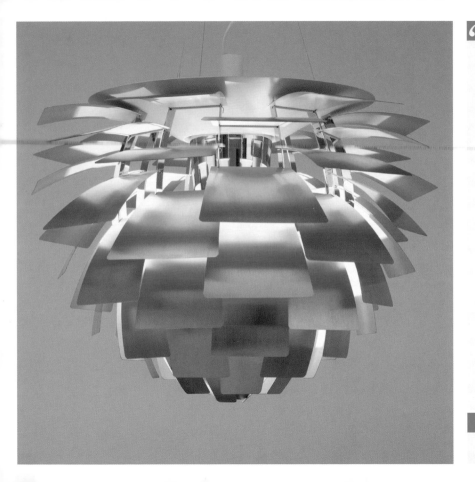

Brushed copper or stainless steel,
paint, lightbulb. Henningsen
maintained, "Light must not blind."

PH Artichoke Lamp 1958
Poul Henningsen

Poul Henningsen created the PH Artichoke lamp for the Langelinie Pavilion restaurant in Copenhagen, Denmark, in 1958. His brief was to produce lighting that was cheery and welcoming, and the lamp he designed in response not only gave a vibrant glow but also generated a warm ambience. The PH Artichoke lamp has seventy-two thin, overlapping, metal leaves that form twelve rows of six, each hanging from a central frame. The positioning of the leaves makes the lamp glare-free from any angle, while still allowing it to radiate light. Made of sheet copper or stainless steel, the pieces are pliant and painted white on their undersides, which creates soft reflections. Before manufacturing his expressive lighting, Henningsen made numerous scientific studies. This design, in particular, meets his goal of producing a lamp that emits a gentle and harmonious light, thereby recalling the oil lamps of his childhood.

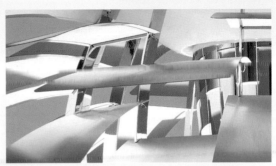

Although it was designed originally as a large and luxurious light fitting for a restaurant, the PH Artichoke lamp has since been used in public and private interiors around the world on account of the abundant soft light it disperses and the cozy, relaxing atmosphere it creates. Initially, in Denmark, it was called the "Kogle," or "Pinecone," but it soon became known as the Artichoke, and gained enormous popularity because it complemented both modern and traditional interiors.

Zen Lamp	*Urchin Lamp*	*Sirius Mushroom Hanging Light*	*Crinkle Lamp*
Sergi and Oscar Devesa	**Jonathan Goldman**	**Sirius Designs**	**Lyn Godley and Lloyd Schwan**
1990	1991	1994	1996

 The designer of the iconic Kikkoman soy sauce bottle, Tokyo-born Kenji Ekuan, set out to create a practical, sturdy, easy-clean container that would not increase the price of the product. At the time, Kikkoman's soy sauce was being sold in cans, which made it messy to use, and any leftover product had to be discarded after a few days. Ekuan took three years to design the bottle, and produced more than one hundred prototypes before he came up with the solution: a shapely form that expressed practicality, reliability, and Eastern elegance. Originally designed as part of a condiment set, the bottle manifested the values of the product, thereby creating a unique and recognizable brand identity. Shaped somewhat like a water droplet with a flat bottom, the bottle has been linked through twenty-first-century advertising (left) to the iconic nineteenth-century Japanese woodcut *Under the Wave, off Kanagawa* (c. 1829–1833), by Katsushika Hokusai, firmly establishing it as a classic of Japanese design.

 Glass, plastic, ink. Ekuan's minimalist approach inspired a series of international design trends in packaging.

Kikkoman Soy Sauce Bottle 1961
Kenji Ekuan

I believe that it is the essential purpose of industrial design to serve the people, be they rich or poor."

Kenji Ekuan

The teardrop shape of the Kikkoman soy sauce bottle has become a familiar sight on dining tables around the world. Since Ekuan first introduced the glassware in 1961, more than 300 million bottles have been sold—and the form has not changed since that time. Ekuan's innovative approach inspired a more considered involvement with product design in Japanese industry and also in a wider context, as many international manufacturers began to rethink their product designs to attain the same recognition, appeal, and brand loyalty as Kikkoman. Made of robust, dishwasher-safe glass, the vessel is refillable and virtually unbreakable. With its distinctive flat red top, graceful curves, simple gold lettering, and spout that does not drip, the Kikkoman soy sauce bottle endures as both a modern-looking and practical container.

Colman's Mustard Pot
J. and J. Colman
1823

Heinz Tomato Ketchup Bottle
Henry Heinz
1890

Condensed Soup Can
Joseph Campbell
1898

Quaker Oats Round Box
Henry Parsons Crowell
1915

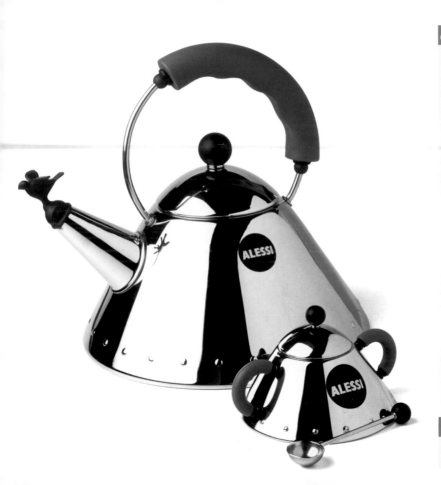

> *It was important to keep both the human aspects and the machine in mind. What looks good also often feels good."*
> **Michael Graves**

Stainless steel, polyamide. In line with other postmodernists, Graves believed in bringing personality back into design.

Whistling Tea Kettle 1985
Michael Graves

One of the icons of postmodernism, this tea kettle, known for its bird that "sings" when the water boils, references the Art Deco styles that were popular fifty years before it was made. U.S. architect Michael Graves was commissioned by Italian manufacturer Alessi to create a non-electric tea kettle that would boil quickly and that looked American. Graves immediately worked out that the first condition could be achieved by employing a wide base, whereas the second could be managed by creating a shape that resembled the Art Deco styles of the Jazz Age. The noisy spout also recalled stove-top tea kettles, which whistled when the water boiled, but by adding the little red plastic bird, the designer was also giving rein to a free and humorous form of expression. Postmodernists often referred to the past, creating new objects out of earlier styles, and the immediate success of this tea kettle meant that Graves went on to design a range of coordinating products, including a sugar bowl and teaspoon.

Reminiscent of children's toys and contrasting with the blue plastic handle, the little red bird whistles when steam from the boiling water rushes up the spout. The bird has to be removed in order to pour the water, and it is not an essential component of the kettle. This reflects the postmodernist tenet that form often takes preference over function. With its simple contours, restrained use of materials, and charming wit, the whistling tea kettle was one of Alessi's most successful designs.

Hot Bertaa Kettle	*Electric Kettle*	*Millennium Kettle*	*Cordless Kettle*
Philippe Starck	**Kenneth Grange for Kenwood**	**Russell Hobbs**	**Jasper Morrison for Rowenta**
1989	1994	1997	2004

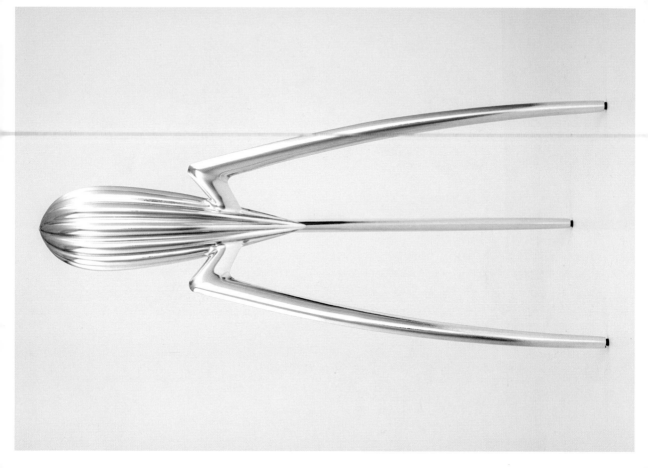

Juicy Salif Citrus Squeezer 1990
Philippe Starck

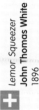

Realizing the importance of innovation and novelty value for consumer products, Starck created his unique, cutting-edge citrus juicer, which looked nothing like a conventional lemon squeezer. He noted: "[It was] not meant to squeeze lemons [but] to start conversations." Alberto Alessi, founder of the Alessi company, recalled: "I received a napkin from Starck... there were some sketches ... they took on the unmistakable shape of what was to become the Juicy Salif."

The Juicy Salif was created by French designer Philippe Starck for Italian manufacturer Alessi, and its name derives from the French word for saliva (salive). Unlike previous lemon squeezers, it was expressive, witty, and more ornamental than functional. While not satisfying the requirements of most juicers—the pointed legs seem precarious; there is no spout, no lip to catch the juice, and no strainer for the seeds and pith—it met the postmodernist philosophy of allowing form to supersede function. Three long tapering legs extend downward, leaving space for a small glass, while the body of the juicer adds to its zoomorphic impression. With its futuristic design, the Juicy Salif epitomized domestic kitchens of the late twentieth century.

" *When I design,*
I don't consider
the technical
or commercial
parameters so
much as the desire
for a dream that
humans have
attempted to project
onto an object."
Philippe Starck

Lemon Squeezer
John Thomas White
1896

Multipress Citrus Juicer
Dieter Rams and Jürgen
Greubel for Braun 1972

Cast and polished aluminum. An icon of industrial design, the Juicy Salif divides consumer opinion.

MOVEMENT

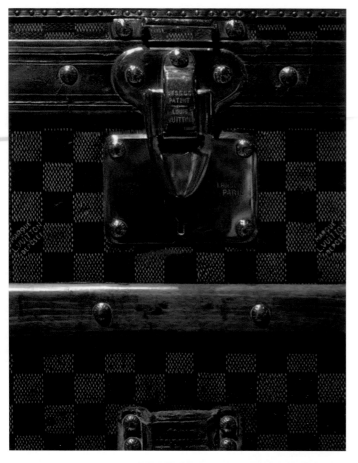

In 1852, having assumed the title Emperor of the French, Napoleon III commissioned Louis Vuitton to make travel boxes for his wife's crinolines. Every time she traveled, Empress Eugénie charged Vuitton with "packing the most beautiful clothes in an exquisite way." Soon, her elite friends flocked to secure Vuitton's box-making services for themselves, and, in 1854, he founded his own luxury box-making and packing workshop in Paris. The sign outside his shop read: "Securely packs the most fragile objects. Specializing in packing fashions." Four years later, Vuitton launched an entirely new trunk for travelers. Instead of traditional leather, it was made of canvas coated with glue, which was lighter, more durable, and waterproof. It was also flat-topped, which contrasted with conventional round-topped trunks, so it could be stacked for greater convenience when being moved from place to place.

Louis Vuitton trunk, 1890, made of vinylized canvas, leather, oak, and brass. Since 1959, the company has used its individual method of coating canvas in PVC.

Trunk 1858
Louis Vuitton

> *It took me years to work out what was so special about Vuitton. But when you go to the workshops outside Paris and see how everything is crafted, it's pretty impressive."*

Marc Jacobs
fashion designer

In 1867, Vuitton modified his trunk design to deter imitators, and, in 1888, he created the *damier* (checkerboard) canvas pattern, with the logo "marque L. Vuitton déposée" or "L. Vuitton registered trademark" on every trunk. After Vuitton's death in 1892, his son, Georges, continued the momentum with international patents, unique combination locks, and, in 1896, the monogram canvas pattern featuring symbols such as quatrefoils and the LV monogram. The brand's luxury image has been secured by upmarket advertisements, such as one for Louis Vuitton luggage (right), photographed in Greenwich Village, New York, in the mid-1950s.

| *Rayée Canvas Trunk*
Louis Vuitton
1876–1888 | *Damier Canvas Trunk*
Louis Vuitton
1888 | *Folding Trunk*
BelMal Malletier
1890 | *Monogram Canvas Trunk*
Louis Vuitton
1896 |

 The drawback of the original "shank-and-worm" corkscrew, which had been around since at least the seventeenth century, was that it had to be pulled out with considerable force. Then, in April 1888, Neville Heeley of James Heeley & Sons in Birmingham, England, patented the first successful "double lever" mechanical corkscrew. The simple movements of raising the arms, turning the worm (screw) into the cork, and then lowering the arms enabled any cork to be extracted from a bottle with minimum effort. Nickel plating made the corkscrew extremely hard wearing and improved the strength of the levers. In addition, the simplicity of Heeley's design enabled it to be mass-produced easily and economically. Known as the A1 double lever corkscrew, it was manufactured for more than sixty years.

 Copper paint, nickel-plate. Heeley's design was the first successful double lever corkscrew.

A1 Double Lever Corkscrew 1888
Neville Heeley

> *Here's to the corkscrew—a useful key to unlock the storehouse of wit, the treasury of laughter, the front door of fellowship, and the gate of pleasant folly."*
>
> **W. E. P. French**
> writer

Heeley's A1 double lever corkscrew improved on an earlier model by another designer, William Baker, also for the James Heeley & Sons manufacturing company. Although Baker's design had two levers, they worked individually and therefore made the device awkward to use. In Heeley's design, the frame fits comfortably onto the neck of a bottle, and the guide disk joining the two pivotal arms makes the arm movement smooth and almost effortless. It also helped to facilitate the insertion and rotation of the worm into the cork. Countless corkscrew designs were available at the time (right), but Heeley's was the most efficient.

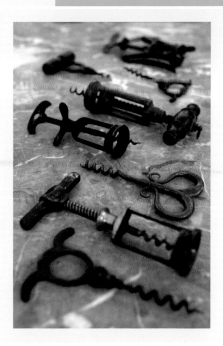

Woodman's Patent Corkscrew
Wilbur B. Woodman
1886

French Express Corkscrew
Jacques Perille
1899

Neues Patent Swinging Frame Corkscrew **Eduard Becker**
1903

Le Parfait Corkscrew
Victor Rousseau
1905

KitchenAid Food Mixer 1930s
Egmont Arens

Perceived as a status symbol in any kitchen, the original multifunctional Model K had various attachments that were easily secured and removed, in order to facilitate the making of bread, pastry, waffles, pasta, and more. The machine's powerful revolutions were also unique for the time: the attachment rotates around its own axis, resulting in greater contact with ingredients and more comprehensive mixing, beating, kneading, and whisking. Aesthetically designed so that the inner curve of the mixer closely follows the contours of the mixing bowl, the Model K was so popular that it sold out at every Christmas for the first few years after its launch. Other colors were available from 1955.

In the early 1930s, the Hobart Manufacturing Company—now known as KitchenAid—commissioned U.S. industrial designer Egmont Arens to design a series of affordable food mixers for general use. Within a few years, the KitchenAid Model K stand mixer designed by Arens was introduced. From the moment it was launched, the Model K was sought after by professional cooks and bakers, as well as by ordinary housewives. Not only did the machine look sleek, modern, and practical, but also the mixer parts moved smoothly, efficiently, and relatively quietly.

> *If you create a product which you hope to sell and want to ensure its acceptance by the public, make sure the various parts are organized into a trim, sleek, streamlined shape."*
> **Egmont Arens**

Model K5SS, 1978: aluminum, stainless steel. The first Model K was produced only in white.

Sunbeam Mixmaster
Ivar Jepson
1930

Kenwood Chef
Kenneth Wood
1950

Kitchen Machine
**Gerd Alfred Müller
for Max Braun** 1957

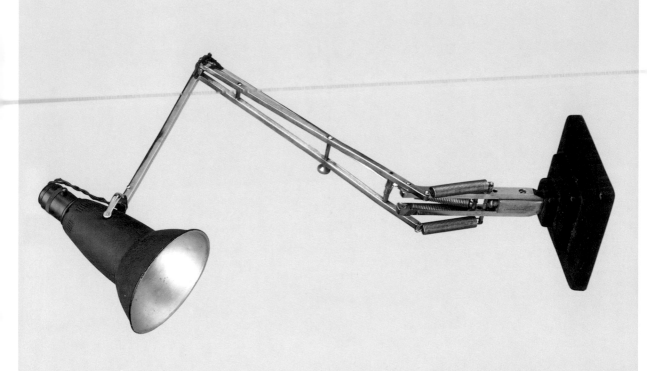

Anglepoise Lamp 1933
George Carwardine

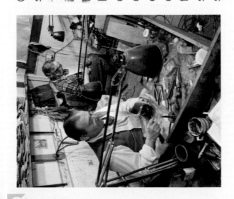

Carwardine created his Anglepoise lamp specifically for close work at workshops and factories, for example at the John Lobb shoe factory [left]. However, his spring supplier, Herbert Terry & Sons, realized that the lamp would be equally suitable for offices and homes. A key feature of its versatile adjustability is the placement of the springs—either three or four—near the base, elbow, and top. These enable the lamp to be moved to almost any position, and the reflective surface inside the shade intensifies the light, so a low-wattage bulb can be used.

Sturdy and flexible, the Anglepoise lamp can be adjusted to different heights by means of counterbalanced springs, and held in those positions without clamps or counterweights. In the early 1930s, English engineer George Carwardine, who specialized in designing vehicle suspension systems, developed a spring that could be moved easily in all directions, yet held each position rigidly. He patented the spring in 1932, then set about finding a suitable use for it. Designed in 1933 and first produced in 1934, his Anglepoise lamp had a heavy tiered base, metal shade, and spindly arm held by his unique and versatile springs.

The Anglepoise is a minor miracle of balance. . . . Balance is a quality in life that we do not value as we should."

Kenneth Grange
industrial designer

Three spring-and-lever mechanism, aluminum, steel, wire.

Emeralite Lamp
Harrison D. McFaddin
1909

Jazz Desk Lamp
Ferdinand Porsche
1989

Half Brogue Oxford 1937
John Lobb

Brogues were originally made in Scotland and Ireland, where the perforations enabled water to drain when the wearer was crossing wet, marshy terrain. John Lobb Ltd.'s Half Brogue Oxfords, however, were created specifically for gentlemen to wear in almost any context. Also known as semi-brogues, the shoes feature decorative perforations and serrations along the toecap, edges, and laces, and around the heel. They were the first shoes designed for the modern man that combined comfort and style, appropriate for wearing both formally and informally.

After making his fortune in Australia, initially producing boots for miners, John Lobb returned to London in 1866. Gaining awards for his footwear and a royal warrant, he attracted a wide international following, which established the reputation of his business. In 1937, his descendant, another John Lobb, designed the Half Brogue Oxford, a lightweight shoe for fancy, but not strictly formal, occasions. Brogues (from the Old Norse word *brók* for "leg-covering") are a style of low-heeled shoe or boot. Oxfords—also known as Balmorals or Richelieu shoes—are a type of lace-up shoe. The Half Brogue Oxford combines elements of both shoes, with specific decorative elements.

Wearing my powder-blue suit with dark blue shirt, tie and display handkerchief, black brogues . . . I was everything the well-dressed private detective ought to be."
Raymond Chandler
writer

Leather, laces. Every pair of shoes is made by several specialized craftsmen.

Oxfords
Church's
1873

Oxfords
Crockett & Jones
1879

Chester Brogue
John Loake
1880s

> **"** *The most durable raw materials are not cement, wood, stone, iron, steel, aluminum, pottery or glass: but art."*
> **Giò Ponti**

Triple-plated chrome steel, pump. This was the first espresso machine with a horizontal boiler for smoother coffee.

La Pavoni Coffee Machine 1948
Giò Ponti

La Pavoni had been producing coffee machines since the early twentieth century, when, in 1947, Giò Ponti was asked to design a new one for the company. Ponti worked with designers Antonio Fornaroli and Alberto Rosselli to create a type of boiler that moved water through pressure over the coffee, and prevented the burned flavor that was common with other coffee machines. Ponti's design resulted in a much less fussy mechanism than that used in other industrial coffee makers. His sleek, shiny chrome machine was the first of its kind to be marketed worldwide, and it was bought as much abroad as in Italy. As a result, La Pavoni disseminated the 1950s fashion for drinking Italian-style coffee in bars and cafés. Curvaceous and stylish, Ponti's La Pavoni machine was called "La Cornuta" (The Horn) after its shape, although it was soon nicknamed the "chrome peacock" for its resplendent appearance.

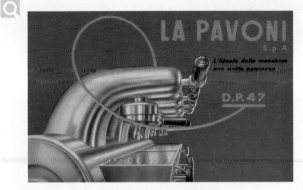

The organically shaped, highly reflective La Cornuta, officially called the DP47, is often referred to as the most beautiful of all industrial espresso machines. In its advertising (above), it was made clear that water flowed through it efficiently, resulting in smoother, better tasting coffee. In his publicity, Ponti declared: "We have been able to satisfy the desire of our clients to exercise complete control over the coffee-making process."

Espresso Coffee Machine	*Espresso Coffee Machine*	*Espresso Coffee Machine*	*E61*
Angelo Moriondo	**Luigi Bezzera**	**Achille Gaggia**	**Faema**
1884	1906	1938	1961

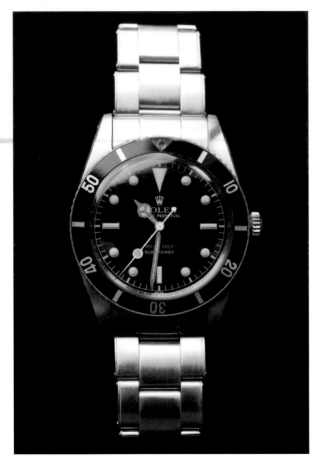

 [The heart is] just a muscle. Only it is the main muscle. It works as perfectly as a Rolex Oyster Perpetual. The trouble is you cannot send it to the Rolex representative when it goes wrong. When it stops, you just do not know the time. You're dead."

Ernest Hemingway
writer

Stainless steel, crystal glass, nitrogen-alloyed steel, grade 5 titanium, and radium paint. A first-rate marketing man, Hans Wilsdorf originated the modern concept of celebrity testimonials.

In 1905, German-born Hans Wilsdorf founded a watch importing company with his brother-in-law, Alfred Davis. He registered the company's name as Rolex, and, in 1926, Rolex produced the world's first waterproof watch case, which Wilsdorf called the Oyster. Hermetically sealed, the Rolex Oyster was guaranteed to remain working in depths of up to 330 feet (100 m). Within a decade, Rolex had also perfected its Perpetual movement, a self-winding mechanism that relied on the wrist motion of the wearer. In 1954, the Rolex Oyster Perpetual Submariner watch was launched, guaranteed to remain waterproof in depths of up to 660 feet (200 m), which was something no other watch company had achieved.

With its famed perpetuity, endurance in extreme depths and temperatures, moving bezel for accurate time-tracking underwater, and flip-lock clasp, the Submariner was designed for divers. Then, during the 1960s, after it was seen on the wrist of 007 in nine James Bond movies, including *Dr. No* (1962; above), it attracted huge prestige among the public. Later models remained watertight in depths of up to 1,000 feet (300 m), and the Submariner became coveted as both a divers' and a gentlemen's classic watch.

Patek Philippe Calatrava
Patek Philippe
1932

Heuer Seafarer (Mareograph)
TAG Heuer
1950

Breitling Superocean
Breitling
1957

Omega Automatic Seamaster
Omega
1960

Rubik's Cube® 1974
Ernö Rubik

The simplicity of the Rubik's Cube—in appearance, concept, and usability—enhanced its fascination across a wide global demographic. The challenge of how fast a person could complete a sequence of moves and return the cube to its original state has become the subject of world records. Some people have become so quick at solving the puzzle that they are known as "speedcubers." Such was the universal appeal of the design that it has influenced other fields such as architecture: the Stadtbibliothek Stuttgart (Stuttgart Library), Germany, designed in 2011 by Korean architect Eun Young Yi, resembles a huge, two-toned Rubik's Cube.

Originally called the Magic Cube, the Rubik's Cube was designed by Hungarian sculptor and professor of architecture Ernö Rubik. He wanted a working model to help explain 3D geometry and ended up creating the world's best-selling toy. With its six colors on fifty-four small cubes, it is easily manipulated. The idea of the puzzle is to jumble the colors by randomly twisting the cubes, and then to rearrange them back into solid color blocks. An internal pivot mechanism enables the outer cubes (only the corners and edges can be moved) to turn independently, through 360 degrees, so the colors can be mixed, displaced, and reordered.

Once I completed the cube and demonstrated it to my students, I realized it was nearly impossible to put down."
Ernö Rubik

Thermoplastic, vinyl stickers, rivets, springs. Sales of the cube peaked between 1980 and 1983.

15-Puzzle
Noyes Palmer Chapman
1874

Nichols Cube Puzzle
Larry D. Nichols
1957

Jenga
Leslie Scott
1982

IMPACT

Cosmos Silver Tea and Coffee Set 1915
Johan Rohde

When Rohde designed this service, he was developing his own sinuous style that built on Art Nouveau. Although he explored some of the ideas of Art Deco and modernism, he did not adopt their newer, more geometric forms. With their streamlined, graceful contours, shiny surfaces, and minimal decoration, his designs became classics almost instantly. The Cosmos service, which included a tray, pitcher, tea and coffee pots, and a covered sugar bowl, was enhanced aesthetically and functionally with fruitwood handles, seamless curves, and organically shaped spouts.

In 1904, Johan Rohde was employed by renowned designer Georg Jensen at his silversmithing workshop in Copenhagen. Jensen was inspired by the Arts and Crafts and Art Nouveau styles, and his work sold extremely well. He admired Rohde's particularly impactful, sleek designs, exemplified by the silver Cosmos tea and coffee service. It is an elegant example of the restraint of contemporary Danish design and of Jensen's influence. The organic curves and ovoid, elongated shapes derive from Art Nouveau, the fluting from antique styles, and the polished surface reflects the incipient reductive modernist style.

> *Do not follow fashion but be guided by the present if you want to stay young in the struggle."*
>
> **Georg Jensen**
> silversmith

 Sterling silver, fruitwood. Minimal embellishments include hammering on the silver.

Silver Tea Service
Archibald Knox
1904–1905

Silver Thistle Coffee Service
Harald Nielsen
1927

Silver Coffee Service
Sigvard Bernadotte
1931

Chrome-plated steel, canvas. The
Wassily chair was initially available
in folding and non-folding versions.

Wassily Chair 1925
Marcel Breuer

Almost as soon as it opened in 1919, the Bauhaus school In Germany became the center of modernist and functional design. Marcel Breuer studied in the carpentry workshop from 1920 to 1924, and in 1925, he took charge of the furniture workshop. For some time he had been preoccupied with the challenge of designing a cantilevered chair that could be mass-produced and made from the same tubular steel as the handlebars of his Adler bicycle. With its shiny frame and suspended sides, back, and seat, the Model B3 chair was the result. Later, when his colleague Wassily Kandinsky admired it, Breuer made one for him, after which the B3 became known as the Wassily chair. Lightweight, resilient, and inexpensive, it was one of the first items of furniture to exploit the potential of tubular steel, and it had a huge impact on contemporary furniture designers, as well as on modernism in general.

Unusually light and easy to assemble from canvas or leather and pre-prepared steel tubes, the Wassily chair has a hammock-like construction, giving users the impression of hovering in the air. With its quintessential structure and composition, it was acclaimed as inspirational. The unique creation was only possible at that time because a German steel manufacturer had recently perfected a process for making seamless steel tubing—previously, steel tubing had to be made with a welded seam that often collapsed when it was bent.

Model S33 Chair
Mart Stam
1927

MR10 Tubular Steel Chair
Ludwig Mies van der Rohe
1927

Model B34 Armchair
Marcel Breuer
1928

Utility Side Chair
Stephen Povey
1986

LC4 Chaise Longue 1928
Le Corbusier, Pierre Jeanneret, and Charlotte Perriand

The LC4 chaise longue is one of three chairs designed concurrently by Le Corbusier, Jeanneret, and Perriand. With its blend of elegance, functionalism, symmetry, and asymmetry, it adhered to Le Corbusier's stipulation "for relaxation." Traditionally, the framework of large items of furniture was concealed by upholstery, but the frame of the LC4 was purposefully exposed and intrinsic to the design. Light and practical, the tubular steel is evocative of a machine; however, ergonomics was also a crucial feature. The recliner rests freely on the black steel legs, and the cushioned neck-roll can be adjusted for comfort.

The LC4 chaise longue, also known as the B306, is one of the purest expressions of modernist furniture. A collaboration between architects Le Corbusier, his cousin Pierre Jeanneret, and Charlotte Perriand, it was inspired by eighteenth-century day beds, but its shape, smooth upholstery, and chromo-plated tubular steel base complied with Le Corbusier's restrained machine-age aesthetic. While its visual impact was arresting, the chair was also comfortable because it followed the shape of the body. Le Corbusier called it "the true resting machine."

I thought of the cowboy from the Wild West smoking his pipe, feet in the air higher than his head . . . complete rest"
Le Corbusier

Chrome-plated steel, black lacquer, steel springs, rubber, leather or pony hide.

MR10 Tubular Steel Chair
Ludwig Mies van der Rohe
1927

Grand Confort, LC2 Club Chair
Le Corbusier, Pierre Jeanneret, Charlotte Perriand 1928

Lockheed Lounge
Marc Newson
1986

> *Build your product with integrity, stand behind it one hundred percent, and success will follow."*
> **George G. Blaisdell**

Chrome-plated brass, flint, wick, fuel. Blaisdell called his lighter "Zippo" because it sounded modern and stylish.

Zippo Lighter 1933
George G. Blaisdell

Virtually unchanged since it was first designed, the Zippo lighter was inspired by a friend of its designer. George G. Blaisdell had asked the friend why he was using a windproof but rather unwieldy lighter. The reply was, "Well, George, it works." From that moment, Blaisdell determined to create an attractive, affordable lighter that was guaranteed to work under almost any conditions. Within a year, he had made and marketed his Zippo lighter with the motto: "It works or we fix it for free." With its smooth, rectangular shape, spring-loaded flip top, and protective windshield, the Zippo was cleverly designed and had an immediate impact.

Blaisdell obtained a patent for his Zippo lighter in 1936, but its reputation for reliability was established when the United States entered World War II in 1941. The designer dedicated his entire production run to the U.S. military, making the lighter in steel rather than brass, with a black crackle finish. Stories abound of Zippos in soldiers' pockets deflecting potentially fatal bullets, and of them being used to heat soup in upturned helmets. The Zippo has also been seen in numerous movies, such as *Never So Few* (1959), in which Frank Sinatra (left) starred as a soldier fighting in Burma.

Banjo Lighter
Ronson Lighter Company
1926

Abdulla Lighter
Abdulla & Company Ltd
c. 1930

Alluma Lady
Colibri
c. 1934

BIC Disposable Lighter
Flaminaire Design Team for BIC
1973

133

Fiesta Dinnerware 1936
Frederick Hurten Rhead

Ceramic, colored glaze.
Concentric curving ridges
are the only decoration.

The name "Fiesta" epitomized the light-heartedness of Rhead's range of tableware, with its vibrant colors and congruent Art Deco shapes. The original five colors were red, cobalt-blue, green, yellow, and ivory, but as fashions changed, a softer palette was introduced while the harmonious shapes remained constant. The line was an instant success; by its second year of production, more than one million pieces of Fiesta dinnerware had been produced.

Color! That's the trend today . . . plates of one color . . . contrasting cups and saucers . . . it's fun to set a table with Fiesta!"
Homer Laughlin China Company brochure

Born in England, Frederick Hurten Rhead emigrated to the United States as a young man and worked as a potter. Within a few years, he was hired as art director of Homer Laughlin China Company in West Virginia, where he produced a range of colorful glazed dinnerware called Fiesta. Initially created in five colors, it was designed for customers to mix and match. The concept was not new, but the line made an instant impact and was soon expanded. Reflecting the prevalent Art Deco styles, it was affordable and bright, with smooth, rounded shapes and vivid colored glazes. Although launched during the Depression, Fiesta was one of the best-selling lines of dinnerware in the United States.

Cornishware
T. G. Green & Co.
1926

American Modern
Russel Wright
1937

Polarized tempered glass, stainless steel, plastic. U.S. Army test pilot F. W. Hunter sports Ray-Ban Aviators in 1942.

Ray-Ban Aviator Sunglasses 1937
Bausch & Lomb

Although sunglasses were first made in about 1885, they were not widely worn. Then, in the 1930s, Ray-Ban Aviators were created to protect the eyes of pilots from the sun's glare, eventually inspiring a new fashion in eyewear. Airplanes were built to fly higher and farther than ever before, and many pilots experienced headaches and altitude sickness as a result. John A. Macready of the U.S. Army Air Corps asked the New York–based eye health company Bausch & Lomb if it could make sunglasses for the pilots, and, by 1936, it had produced "anti-glare" sunglasses with plastic frames and green lenses that reduced dazzle without obscuring vision. Remodeled with a metal frame in 1937, the sunglasses were launched as "Ray-Ban Aviators," to associate them with their purpose. Immediately, pilots from across the world began wearing them. A year later, Ray-Ban started selling Aviators to the public, and the impact of being seen worn by celebrities in the 1960s imbued them with distinction.

Covering an area much larger than the eye, Ray Ban Aviator lenses are slightly convex, absorbing 85 percent of visible light and reducing glare. Thin metal frames encircle the distinctive teardrop shape, while flexible temples hook comfortably behind the ears. The ultimate goal of these uniquely curved glasses was to shield the eyes from every angle for optimal protection from the sun, but they also became firmly established as stylish and glamorous eyewear.

Ray-Ban Wayfarers	Model 649	Oakley	Wiley X
Bausch & Lomb	**Persol**	**Jim Jannard**	**Protective Optics**
1952	1957	1975	1986

Butterfly Stool 1954
Sori Yanagi

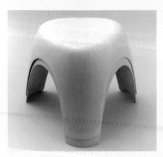

Yanagi's interest in both seating and modernism was probably inspired by architect and designer Charlotte Perriand, who had worked in Le Corbusier's studio in Paris. From 1940 to 1942, Perriand was Japan's official advisor on industrial design, and it was during that time that Yanagi worked as her assistant. In 1952, he founded the Yanagi Industrial Design Institute in Tokyo, where he created his best-known chair designs: the Butterfly stool (opposite) and the Elephant stool (left). Like the Butterfly stool, the Elephant stool, made of glass-fiber polyester resin, is candidly symmetrical. Both seats are modest, effective, and functional. Despite the chairs' modernist leanings, Yanagi worked in a traditional manner, starting with drawings and making prototypes by hand.

Modern in its purity and economy of line, this bent and molded plywood stool exploits the patterned grain of the wood from which it is made. The stool's impact is strikingly simple, yet it fuses a combination of ancient and modern, and Eastern and Western ideas. Sori Yanagi created it from two identical pieces of maple plywood, joined in the center and reinforced with a single metal rod. The butterfly stool has been compared to several things, including calligraphy strokes; *torii*, the gateways that form the approaches to Shinto temples; whale tails; and, of course, butterfly wings.

When you make an object that is to be used by hand, it should be made by hand."
Sori Yanagi

Maple plywood, brass fittings. The stool helped to change Western perceptions of design.

Cross Check Armchair
Frank Gehry for Knoll
1990

Less Stacking Stool
Marco Ferreri for BPA International 1993

Lou Read Chair
Philippe Starck
2011

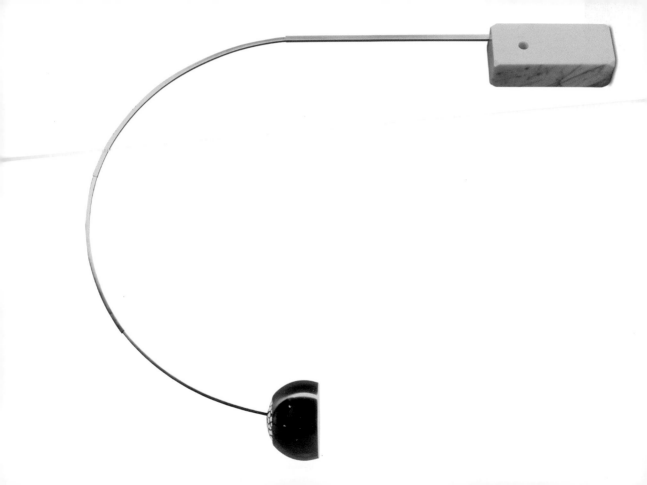

Arco Lamp 1962
Achille and Pier Giacomo Castiglioni

Seeking stylish and functional solutions to various household products, Italian brothers Achille and Pier Giacomo Castiglioni, who had both studied architecture, often collaborated with each other. They became among the most prolific and influential industrial designers of the second half of the twentieth century. In the early 1960s, they considered the problem of lighting a dining table without drilling holes into the walls or ceiling. Originally inspired by street lights, the Arco lamp consisted of a long stainless steel arch made of four pieces of telescopic tubing, a polished dome-shaped shade, and a heavy white marble base. It created a huge impact on contemporary interior design.

Made of marble from the same quarry as that used to create Michelangelo's *David* (1501–1504), the heavy base has both a practical and glamorous purpose. The dramatic, reflective, spherical shade is made of two parts: the cap, perforated to allow heat to escape, and the movable, shiny aluminum shade, which can be tilted to adjust the angle of light. The steel arc contains the wiring, and the extent of its reach augments the lamp's dramatic appeal.

Steel, aluminum, Carrara marble, lightbulb.

> *Start from scratch.*
> *Stick to common*
> *sense. Know your*
> *goals and means."*
> **Achille Castiglioni**

Parentesi Lamp
Achille Castiglioni and Pio Manzù for Flos 1970

Calida Floor Light
Fête Sans
1986

CONVENIENCE

Enameled Cookware 1925
Le Creuset

Although many technological advances have been employed by Le Creuset since its cookware was first made, some original, effective processes continue to be used, such as forging with sand and hand-smoothing, thereby establishing Le Creuset's name for quality and endurance. The pans, which are now available in a wider range of colors, can be used on any heat source, while their precisely fitting lids enclose heat. This makes them energy efficient and versatile, and able to cook different types of food gently and well. Products that have been added to the range include mugs (left), introduced in 2009.

Based on ancient Roman cooking pots and made of enameled cast iron, Le Creuset cookware (French for "the cauldron") was invented by two Belgians, Armand Desaegher (a casting specialist) and Octave Aubecq (an enameling specialist), and it has been produced at Fresnoy-le-Grand in France since 1925. The range of cookware has a double enamel coating, fired at 1,544°F (840°C), which makes the pots especially resilient and durable. Using a new method of coloring the enamel glaze, Desaegher and Aubecq created their signature color "flame" to reflect the orange hue of molten cast iron inside a cauldron.

Every cook should know a little French. Le Creuset."
U.S. advertising slogan (1980)

Cast iron, porcelain enamel. The cookware is still forged using the original wet sand method.

Pyrex Glassware
Corning Incorporated
1915

Dansk Kobenstyle
Jens Quistgaard
1956

Calphalon Cookware
Ronald Kasperzak
1963

 After he had produced the Wassily chair in 1925, Marcel Breuer designed the B32 chair, which became known as the "Cesca" in the 1960s, after his daughter, Francesca. Functional, light, and convenient, it used cane, beechwood, and cantilevered tubular steel. Without legs, the cantilevering relied on the tensile properties of the steel tubing, making it pliant and meeting Breuer's ideal that chairs should feel like "sitting on columns of air." The lengths of industrial-looking chromed tubular steel did not borrow from any past styles, and the chair seemed to be completely original. However, Breuer had designed it a year after designers Mart Stam and Ludwig Mies van der Rohe had introduced their cantilevered chairs to the public. This resulted in a complex series of lawsuits, and the B32 was not manufactured until 1930. Although Breuer ceased designing with tubular steel after this, from 1933 to 1936 he manufactured the B64, the armchair version of the B32, with metal arms attached above the seat.

 Chrome-plated steel, beechwood, cane. Although the Cesca was arguably not the first cantilevered steel chair, there is no doubt that it was the first successful "legless" chair.

Cesca Chair 1928
Marcel Breuer

> *Our guiding principle was that design is neither an intellectual nor a material affair, but simply an integral part of the stuff of life, necessary for everyone in a civilized society."*

Walter Gropius
architect and principal
of the Bauhaus

Three years before Breuer designed the Cesca chair, architect Walter Gropius designed a building for the Bauhaus school in Dessau, Germany. One of the features was a series of cantilevered tubular steel balconies (left). Breuer worked closely with Gropius, and their ideas and vision for simplicity in design were an important part of the Bauhaus. Although Stam and Mies had introduced similar chairs a year before the Cesca appeared, Breuer claimed that he had conceived the idea when turning one of his nesting stools on its side, and had confided it to Stam. If so, this places Breuer as the originator of the cantilevered steel chair.

Cantilever Chair
Mart Stam
1927

E1027 Side Table
Eileen Gray
1927

Armchair 42
Alvar Aalto
1932

Fauteuil 413 RH
William H. Gispen
1933

Moka Express c. 1930
Alfonso Bialetti

Cleverly filtering coffee using heat, the Moka Express was an instant success because it could be used in any kitchen. When heated on a stove, water in the bottom compartment rises via a funnel, up through the coffee grounds in the next section, and then through a filter. Finally, it reaches the top compartment, hot and ready to be poured. Bialetti supposedly designed the pot after observing washing machines, in which soapy water rose as it was heated over a fire.

Italian engineer Alfonso Bialetti established a workshop in his native Piedmont in 1919, specifically to make aluminum products. Influenced by designers such as Josef Hoffmann and Jean Puiforcat, he manufactured the Moka Express coffee maker from a design by engineer Luigi De Ponti. Unique in its use of aluminum, which was cheap and rarely employed for domestic items at that time, the Moka Express was the first coffee machine made for domestic use. Conveniently, it enabled people to make their own espresso at home, rather than having to go to a café. With its symmetrical, eight-faceted, metallic body, it reflected stylish contemporary Art Deco designs, and rapidly became the world's best-known coffee pot.

> *With the reassuring rumble of the coffee being produced over a gas flame, [the Moka] established a connection with the public's imagination."*
>
> **Alberto Alessi**
> Bialetti's grandson

Aluminum and plastic. The handle and knob echo the angular design.

Wigomat Drip Coffee Maker
Gottlob Widmann
1954

Estro Coffee Press
Jørgen Bodum
1974

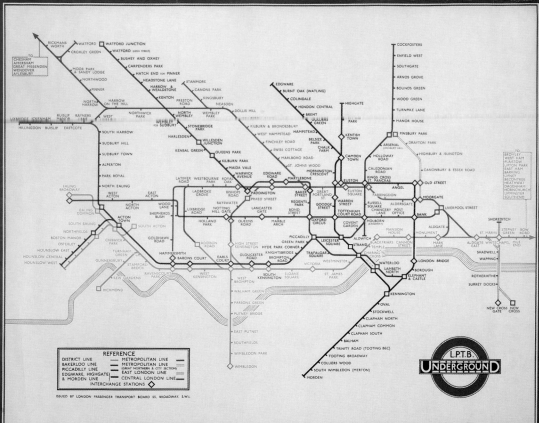

London Underground Map 1933
Harry Beck

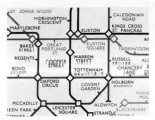

Abandoning geographic accuracy, Beck stripped all extraneous details from his map. Designed on a grid and based on the circuit diagrams that he drew for his day job, Beck's map was coherent and instantly comprehensible, adding to the modern, efficient image that London Underground was trying to promote. The map became an essential guide to the city's subway system, as well as a model for transport maps around the world. It was perceived as one of the great achievements of modernist design, even though Beck knew far more about circuits than he did about art and design.

The original map of the London Underground from 1908 included the streets above and was difficult to interpret. New designs were made in various formats, each attempting to clarify the routes for passengers. The first Underground map without geographic details was designed in 1920, but, because it was still to scale, it remained confusing. Then, in 1931, in his spare time, Harry Beck, an engineering draftsman at the London Underground signals office, created a color-coded diagram map, illustrating plainly how to move from one station to another. The shapes of the routes were simplified, the interchanges were clearly marked, and all stations were more or less equally spaced.

It occurred to me that it might be possible to tidy it up by straightening the lines . . . and evening out the distances between stations."
Harry Beck

Print on paper or card. Within six months of publication, over one million maps were in circulation.

New York Subway Map
Massimo Vignelli
1972

Washington Metro Map
Lance Wyman
2012

Moscow Metro Map
Art. Lebedev Studio
2013

Chrome-plated steel, wood. Loewy took plain, even ugly, consumer items and made them beautiful.

Pencil Sharpener 1933
Raymond Loewy

Applying his streamlining principles to everything from glass bottles and cigarette packets to trains and refrigerators, Raymond Loewy has been called the father of industrial design, "the man who reshaped America." One of his most iconic designs was this sleek, chrome pencil sharpener that resembled the engine of a plane—or a teardrop. Designed for convenience, he invented it during the machine age when sleek Art Deco designs were fashionable and countless machines were being produced with the express purpose of making people's lives easier. Loewy embraced this spirit, creating an object with a rounded front, tapered back, and a handle that both indicates its function and resembles the wing mirror of a car. Although it was a simple piece of office equipment, it was like nothing else used in offices at the time. Loewy believed that good design would clean up the past and help to improve lives over the years following the Great Depression. In the end, however, this pencil sharpener was never put into production.

In his bid to create a completely new look for the United States, Loewy exploited rounded, smooth shapes, created with precision to suggest speed. This is apparent in his pencil sharpener but also in the Pennsylvania Railroad's S1 steam locomotive (above, with Loewy), designed in 1939. The elongated Art Deco shape of the train echoes that of his pencil sharpener and helped to promote a sense of optimism for the future.

Tape Dispenser
John A. Borden for 3M
1932

Rolodex
Arnold Neustadter
1952

Folle 26 Stapler
**Henning Andreasen
for Folle APS** 1977

Dauphine Desktop Calculator
George Sowden for Alessi
1997

ET44 Pocket Calculator 1978
Dieter Rams and Dietrich Lubs

CONVENIENCE
SPEED

Electronic calculators evolved from manual adding machines that were designed in the late nineteenth century by U.S. inventor William Seward Burroughs. He formed the Burroughs Adding Machine Company, which introduced its calculator (left) in c.1911, the design of which was modified over the years. Braun's pocket calculator was developed for the same basic function—simplicity—and ease of use as the Burroughs machine. Jonathan Ive, senior vice president of industrial design at Apple, has long acknowledged Dieter Rams as his inspiration and freely admits that he created some of Apple's icons based on the design of the ET44.

The earliest electronic calculators were extremely expensive, but during the 1970s, integrated circuits and LEDs, rather than the original gas-filled display tubes, were used and prices dropped immediately. Taking advantage of this, Dieter Rams and Dietrich Lubs, working for Braun in Frankfurt, Germany, created a pocket-sized electronic calculator in 1978. Narrow, lightweight, matte, and black, with smooth buttons resembling small shiny beads, the ET44 pocket calculator was conveniently sized to slip in a pocket, and pleasing both to look at and to use. It was also remarkable at the time for the speed with which users could operate it.

In my experience, users react very positively when things are clear and understandable."
Dieter Rams

Plastics, battery, electrical circuits. This Braun calculator is the ET55, from 1980.

Executive Pocket Calculator
Clive Sinclair
1972

HP-35 Scientific Calculator
Hewlett-Packard
1972

Personal Mini Calculator
Casio
1975

Steel, titanium, aluminum, rubber. The central hinge lets the bike fold neatly in half.

Brompton Folding Bicycle 1979
Andrew Ritchie

In 1975, engineer and landscape gardener Andrew Ritchie began designing a folding bike in his apartment in London. He was inspired by the aluminum Bickerton folding bike but believed that a different metal and folding system would be more efficient. With its small wheels, downward-pointing handlebars, and convenient folding mechanism, Ritchie's steel bike, which he called the Brompton, aroused interest among several manufacturers, but they all declined to produce it, believing that no market existed for such a bicycle. So, Ritchie began to make the Brompton himself. Within eighteen months, he had made and sold fifty. Over the next two years, he made and sold hundreds more. Light, strong, and convenient, the bike can be folded and unfolded in approximately ten to twenty seconds. Ritchie incorporated hinges so that the wheels fold inward, enclosing the oily chain and chainwheel.

The design of the Brompton folding bicycle has hardly changed since 1979, when Ritchie filed the original patent. By 1986, he had received sufficient funding to establish his company properly, and it soon became the largest bicycle manufacturer in the United Kingdom. The collapsible Brompton bicycle remains its main product, still functioning efficiently with the same hinged frame and small wheel size that Ritchie designed originally.

Bickerton Portable	*The Stowaway*	*Dahon Jifo*	*Montague BiFrame*
Harry Bickerton	**Raleigh**	**Dahon**	**Harry Montague**
1971	1971	1982	1987

> *Carefully watch how people live, get an intuitive sense as to what they might want and then go with it. . . . It was my intuition that convinced me the Walkman would be a great success."*

Akio Morita
co-chairman,
Sony Corporation

 Anodized aluminum, Plexiglas, plastic. The Walkman irrevocably changed social attitudes toward private music played in public places.

Sony Walkman 1979
Nobutoshi Kihara

In 1963, the Philips electronics company created the first portable cassette recorder for office use. By the late 1960s, other firms were doing the same for the public, but, although compact, the recorders were still fairly cumbersome. Then, in July 1979, the Japanese Sony Corporation, already renowned for its well-designed, miniaturized electronics, introduced the Sony Walkman TPS-L2. Designed by Nobutoshi Kihara, Sony's audio-division engineer, the Walkman was a pocket-sized blue and silver portable cassette player with headphones, a second earphone jack so that two people could listen at once, and a leather case. There was no external speaker, and it ran on two small batteries, making it inexpensive to run and easy to use. Slipped into the pocket, it could be taken almost anywhere, while users listened privately to music of their choice. By 1983, the Sony Walkman was outselling vinyl records for the first time since they had been invented, almost a century before.

The idea for the design of the Sony Walkman began with the company's co-chairman Akio Morita, who wanted to be able to listen to operas during frequent long flights. Kihara produced a prototype for the Walkman in 1978. As soon as it was launched the following year, the Walkman boasted an unprecedented combination of portability and privacy, which attracted thousands of buyers from around the world, of all ages.

Norelco Carry-Corder 150	*MiniDisc*	*iPod*	*Walkman NWZ-X1000*
Philips	**Sony Corporation**	**Jonathan Ive for Apple**	**Sony Corporation**
1964	1992	2001	2009

COMMUNICATION

Meisterstück 149 1924
Montblanc

First produced in 1924, the torpedo-shaped Meisterstück 149 pen became the firm's most successful product. The hand-tested gold and platinum nib is renowned for its clarity, adapting to different handwriting styles and thus facilitating individual interpretation and expression. In recognition of some of the great writers who have used Montblanc, the company produces limited editions, such as the "Agatha Christie" snake pen (left), based on 1920s style.

In 1906, in Hamburg, Germany, three men—engineer August Eberstein, stationer Claus-Johannes Voss, and banker Alfred Nehemias—founded the Simplo Filler Pen Company to manufacture high-quality fountain pens. They produced their first pen in 1909, but it was their second in 1910, that they named Montblanc, after Europe's highest mountain, because the pen was the peak of technical achievement. Montblanc soon became renowned globally for the smooth writing quality of its elegant pens, including the Meisterstück 149 with its hand-crafted nib. Engraved on some Montblanc nibs is the number "4810," which is the height of Mont Blanc mountain in meters, as it was measured at the time.

> *There are a thousand thoughts lying within a man that he does not know till he takes up a pen to write."*
>
> **William Makepeace Thackeray**
> author

+ *Eyedropper Fountain Pen*
Lewis Waterman
c.1903

Lever-filling Fountain Pen
Walter Sheaffer
1913

– Black precious resin, platinum, gold, plastic. The 4810 nib is iconic for its writing qualities.

Leica Camera 1925
Oskar Barnack

Barnack's groundbreaking concept of a lightweight, small-format camera caused a revolution in photography. His portable, compact Leica cameras gave photographers freedom and mobility. Whether amateur or professional, they could concentrate on their subject matter, which generally improved the scope of all genres of photography, from family snaps to art images to reportage. The Leica rapidly became the most popular photo-journalistic camera in the world. Legendary photographer and co-founder of Magnum Photos Henri Cartier-Bresson (left) was well known for using only one camera—a Leica Rangefinder—and a single 50mm lens. The small camera allowed him to "capture the moment" without being noticed by his subjects.

Precision engineer Oskar Barnack designed microscopes for Ernst Leitz Optical Works in Germany. Privately, in 1913, he began building a compact camera for film that produced smaller negatives than any previous film. In order to achieve this, he used negatives on a spool rather than heavy plates. The resulting photographs were of exceptional quality for the time. In 1925, the first Leica camera, named for "Leitz camera," was introduced to the public, instantly communicating that the medium of photography was now accessible to all. By 1932, about 90,000 Leicas were in use worldwide.

Shooting with a Leica is like a long tender kiss . . . like an hour on the analyst's couch."

Henri Cartier-Bresson
photographer

Aluminum, brass, glass, synthetic leather. The Leica I featured interchangeable lenses.

Kodak Box Camera
George Eastman Kodak
1888

No. 2 Beau Brownie
Walter Dorwin Teague for Kodak 1930

Olympus Trip 35
Olympus Design Team
1968

Bakelite (molded phenol
formaldehyde), stainless steel,
woven cloth.

EKCO AD 65 Radio 1934
Wells Coates

Early wireless sets often resembled furniture, but Eric Kirkham Cole of E. K. Cole Ltd. (EKCO), a British electronics company that produced mainly radio and television sets, challenged designers to modernize their traditional appearances. Designs were submitted by Serge Chermayoff, Raymond McGrath, Jesse Collins, Misha Black, and Wells Coates, whose circular radio was selected and marketed as the EKCO AD 65. Abandoning any historical or decorative details in favor of an unadorned, modern design, the EKCO AD 65 boldly communicated its function. The round shape did not hide the radio behind cabinetwork, and the new and inexpensive, moldable synthetic material Bakelite was used, which fulfilled Coates's desire for "purpose related to purse." The radio was available in black, ivory, and green, as well as the popular brown version that simulated burr walnut, and its Art Deco shape influenced radio design for decades.

The strong visual appeal of modern radios, such as the Philco 444 (1936; above), was perfectly timed as they became an important part of people's lives. Featuring chrome grilles and large dials, EKCO's new, articulate radios discarded all conventions. Their design emphasized their function and simultaneously reduced materials, components, and costs. Several variations of the EKCO AD 65 were made over the following decade.

Pye Radio Model MM	*Volksempfänger VE301*	*Bush DAC90A*	*EKCO U122*
Harold John Pye for	**Otto Griessing**	**Bush**	**E. K. Cole Ltd.**
W. G. Pye 1931	1933	1950	1950

> **"** [If] people are made safer, more comfortable, more eager to purchase, more efficient, or just happier, the designer has succeeded."
>
> **Henry Dreyfuss**

i Thermoplastic, steel, Bakelite (molded phenol formaldehyde), ceramic, cord, leather.

Model 302 Telephone 1937
Henry Dreyfuss

In 1930, U.S. industrial designer Henry Dreyfuss began working with Bell Laboratories. Seven years later, he produced the Model 302 telephone, with a handset and rotary dial designed specifically for comfort, grip, and ease of communication. Strong, utilitarian, and stylish, the telephone was initially made from cast zinc, and later thermoplastic, and the original version came in black only. The Model 302 was the first popular telephone and it continued in production until 1954. Dreyfuss believed in creating products that were based on what he called "the human factor," later known as ergonomics.

With its shape, weight, spring-powered dial, and large receiver and transmitter, the Model 302 telephone was designed around intelligibility. Its great success came from Dreyfuss's intense research into its function and use. Later models were produced in a variety of colors in order to appeal to a wider demographic, particularly women. In the 1950s, the Model 302 was replaced by the lightweight plastic Model 500 (left), designed to meet the growing demand for telephones worldwide. This model was made until 1984.

Number 20B Candlestick Telephone **Western Electric** 1904

Tele 150 **GPO (General Post Office)** 1924

Ericofon **Ericsson Company** 1948

Grillo Folding Telephone **Marco Zanuso and Richard Sapper** 1965

> *The design of each element should be thought out in order to be easy to make and easy to repair."*
>
> **Leo Fender**

Ash, maple, nickel-plate, aluminum, vinyl, thermoplastic, nickel-plated steel strings.

Fender Stratocaster 1954
Leo Fender, George Fullerton, and Freddie Tavares

The Fender Stratocaster is a model of electric guitar designed in 1954 by Californian Leo Fender, assisted by designer George Fullerton and draftsman Freddie Tavares. Some of the greatest rock and pop musicians in the world have played it, including Jimi Hendrix (opposite), Eric Clapton, and John Lennon. With its unique curving shape and rich sound, the "Strat" has become one of the most recognizable electric guitars in the world. Initially, Fender asked musicians what they wanted in their ideal guitar. He was told that lightness, comfort, and a good sound were imperative. Some also wanted an instrument that could be easily maintained and customized. Consequently, Fender built a lightweight guitar with comfortable contours and double cutaways, which made it easy for players to reach all the frets.

Among the inventive and original features of the Fender Stratocaster are three magnetic pickups that capture the vibrations of the strings, a distinctive horn, a "tremolo" arm to alter the pitch while playing, and a sleekly curving silhouette with double cutaways by the neck. The unusual aspect emphasized the guitar's characteristic sound. Completely different in appearance to contemporary guitars, the first Stratocasters were made of ash with a bolted-on maple neck and a black and yellow sunburst finish— red was added later to amplify the effect. Later still, modifications were made using bright paint and individual decorations.

Fender Telecaster
Leo Fender
1950

Gibson Les Paul **Ted McCarty, Les Paul, and The Gibson Guitar Corporation** 1952

Gibson Flying V
The Gibson Guitar Corporation 1958

Rickenbacker 330
Rickenbacker
1958

Steel plate, aluminum, ashwood, plastic. The Braun SK4 deliberately recalled Bauhaus designs.

Braun SK4 1956
Dieter Rams

As head of design at German consumer electronics manufacturer Braun, Dieter Rams produced hundreds of products over a period of forty years. He was inspired by designer and architect Hans Gugelot, who worked with him in developing the Braun SK4 radio and record player, which was put on the market in 1956. Focusing on ease and enjoyment of use, Rams housed the SK4 in a white metal case with two light wooden sides, instead of the heavy wooden casing that was more usual for such objects. He also placed the operating panel on the top, next to the turntable, communicating instantly to the user how to operate the machine. Another unique addition was the transparent plastic lid, which gave an overall clean appearance, although it was not known how consumers would react to this innovation. Attracting the somewhat dubious nickname of "Snow White's coffin," the SK4 was ultimately perceived as stylish and influenced the look of sound systems for more than twenty years.

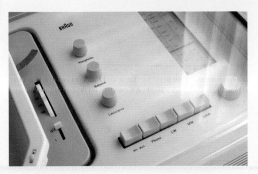

The white plastic controls on the top of the Braun SK4 were easy to clean and did not vibrate as much as metal ones, so the sound was more distinctive than that from other similar machines of the time. Separate loudspeakers also enhanced the sound quality. Renowned contemporary designers such as Jonathan Ive and Jasper Morrison cite Rams and his designs for Braun as a major influence on their work.

Philips AG4049 Portable Record Player
Philips 1960

Dansette Bermuda MK1
Dansette Revolver
1963

Model MK4
Decca Deccalian
1963

Model 22GF
Patrice Dupont for Philips
1969

Unikko Fabric 1964
Maija Isola

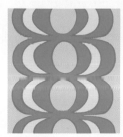

Isola often based her designs on observations from nature. The loose curves that feature in her Unikko print derived from real poppies, although the final graphic pattern is boldly stylized. Her dazzling colors were courageous at the time, as most other fabric designers were producing small, dainty prints in less dramatic colors. In the same year as Unikko, Isola also designed her Kaivo, or "Well" in English, print (left), which came to epitomize the 1960s. This design was inspired when she accidentally dropped a bucket into a well. She became transfixed by the circular ripples on the surface of the water, which continued to radiate for some time. Both Unikko and Kaivo were produced in numerous colorways.

During the 1960s, while she was working for Finnish fabric company Marimekko, Maija Isola revolutionized textile design. Favoring large, vibrant, and dramatic prints, she perfectly communicated the exuberance of the mid-1960s. However, this vivacious pattern, called Unikko, or "Poppy" in English, was nearly not produced, because Armi Ratia, creative director of Marimekko, had declared that the company should not make floral patterns. Isola went ahead and created her bold, flat, floral pattern. After a collection of shift dresses was made in the Unikko print, it became one of the company's best sellers.

Isola was a dangerously original character [who] belonged to a trailblazing generation."
Kaari Utrio
writer

Screen-printed cotton. Isola's design arranges the poppies closely but without overlapping.

Feathers
Alexander Girard
1957

Cockaigne
Lucienne Day
1961

Candy Flower
Celia Birtwell
1968

The eye-catching Valentine portable typewriter consists of two parts: the typewriter itself and its hard plastic carrying case, which slides on effortlessly and forms an exact fit. Designed by Ettore Sottsass and Perry King for Olivetti, an Italian manufacturer of business products, the typewriter broke away from the uninspiring appearance of most other typewriters of the time. Sottsass said: "When I was young, all we ever heard about was functionalism, functionalism, functionalism. It's not enough. Design should also be sensual and exciting." Consequently, he designed the Valentine for portability and convenience, while communicating fun and practicality. It was inspired by Pop art and therefore disassociated from an office environment. The keys are ergonomically designed, and most of the machine is made of brightly colored molded plastic rather than traditional metal. The back incorporates the handle, which slots through the carrying case.

ABS plastic, light steel, aluminum, alloy metals, ribbon. Sottsass said that the Valentine was designed "so as not to remind anyone of monotonous working hours."

Valentine Portable Typewriter 1969
Ettore Sottsass and Perry King

Every color has a history. Red is the color of the Communist flag, the color that makes a surgeon move faster, and the color of passion."

Ettore Sottsass

Despite the vibrant colors—in addition to crimson, the Valentine was also available in white, green, and blue—this portable typewriter was not commercially successful, mainly because the strong colors were thought to cause eye fatigue, and it was expensive. Yet the Valentine has become an iconic design object, epitomizing the 1960s and 1970s, and it was named for the day the typewriter was launched, Valentine's Day, 1969. Advertising for the product was created to resemble works of contemporary Pop art, often featuring romantic couples or young people of the Swinging Sixties (right), reflecting Sottsass's declaration that it was an "anti-machine machine."

Underwood No. 5	Olivetti Studio 42	Selectric 1	Olivetti Lettera 32
Underwood Typewriter Company c.1900	**Olivetti** 1935	**Eliot Noyes for IBM** 1961	**Marcello Nizzoli** 1963

HARMONY

Coca-Cola® Bottle 1915
Earl R. Dean

In 1915, The Coca-Cola Company launched a competition for U.S. manufacturers to design a distinctive bottle that "a person could recognize even if they felt it in the dark." Believing (incorrectly) that "coca" referred to cocoa, Earl R. Dean of the Root Glass Company, Indiana, based his design on a cocoa pod, copied from an encyclopedia. In order to make the shape more harmonious and more stable on a conveyor belt, Dean narrowed the middle bulge and widened the base of his original design (left). The final version, which won the contest, recalled the shapely contours of fashionably dressed women of the time.

Dean's Coca-Cola bottle was different from any other drink containers at the time. Instantly recognizable, with its undulated fluting and embossed lettering, the curvaceous form resembled the hobble skirt, popularized by the designs of Paul Poiret in the early 1900s. As soon as The Coca-Cola Company chose the thick green-glass bottle as the winning entry, it trademarked the design to avoid imitations. Dean created his prototype for the bottle using a cast-iron mold—the Root Glass Company's "Johnny Bull Mold Machine" (left)—in 1915. The father of industrial design, Raymond Loewy, described the contour bottle as "a masterpiece of scientific, functional planning."

Green glass. Coca-Cola requested that the bottle should be identifiable even when broken.

Marble Soft Drink Bottle
Hiram Codd
1872

Perrier Bottle
Dr. Louis Perrier
1898

Evian Bottle
Diane von Furstenberg
2013

Created by German architect Ludwig Mies van der Rohe in collaboration with interior designer Lilly Reich, the Barcelona chair is one of the most iconic designs of the twentieth century. Combining clean lines with contrasting textures, the chair retains an ageless appearance. It was produced as part of Mies's commission to design the entire German Pavilion and its contents for the International Exposition in Barcelona in 1929, and it was one of two made to be used as thrones by the king and queen of Spain in the official opening ceremony. The simple, X-shaped, chrome-plated frame, with its deep, rectangular, leather-covered cushions, perfectly complemented the cool, marble interior of the pavilion.

Chrome-plated flat steel, leather. Mies designed the chair not only to be functional, but also to appear like a sculpture.

Barcelona Chair *c.1929*
Ludwig Mies van der Rohe and Lilly Reich

The long path from material through function to creative work has only one goal: to create order out of the desperate confusion of our time."

Ludwig Mies van der Rohe

A perpetrator of the modernist ideas of the Bauhaus, Mies balanced ancient and modern design styles and materials in his Barcelona chair. As well as utilizing modern substances, such as chrome-plated steel, and creating modernist rectilinear contours, the chair shape and structure were modeled on the *sella curulis*, or curule seat, a stool used originally by ancient Egyptian, Greek, and Roman magistrates. Folding wooden versions of the curule seat (left) were seen in Spain and Italy from the fifteenth century onward. The very clear blending of several design ideas made the Barcelona chair particularly timeless and appealing.

Model No. B302 Swivel Chair
Le Corbusier, Pierre Jeanneret, Charlotte Perriand 1928–1929

Zig-Zag Chair
Gerrit Rietveld
1934

Long Chair
Marcel Breuer
1936

Chair No. 406
Alvar Aalto
1938–1939

Table Clock c. 1929
Albert Cheuret

Silvered bronze was often used for household objects during the 1920s and 1930s to create an impression of luxury and sophistication that was particular to Art Deco. Silver imparted a radiant luster, and Cheuret, who was fascinated with ancient Egyptian art, produced this silvered table clock in the shape of Cleopatra's coiffure. He created numerous other objects, from clocks to furniture to lighting, between the two World Wars, and, in 1925, had his own pavilion at the Paris Exposition internationale des arts décoratifs et industriels modernes, from where the term "Art Deco" derived.

Throughout the 1920s and 1930s, the Art Deco style flourished. Extravagant, angular, and harmonious, it emerged in all forms of design, drawing on tradition while also celebrating the modern world. French sculptor and designer Albert Cheuret designed a range of items at that time, and this shiny clock resembles a fan or the sun's rays, echoing ideas from ancient Egyptian art that had become fashionable after Howard Carter discovered Tutankhamun's tomb in 1922. The decadent style of the clock reflects Art Deco's expression of glamour and exoticism, which modernism avoided, whereas the stylized numbers and geometric face demonstrate directness and simplicity.

Design is . . . about creating forms that accord with the character of the object and that show new technologies to advantage."

Peter Behrens
architect and designer

Silvered bronze, onyx. Cheuret's design gives the impression of solidity and stability.

Clock
C. F. A. Voysey
1895

Mantelpiece Clock
Charles Rennie Mackintosh
1919

Inséparables Clock
René Lalique
c. 1926

*Everything is sculpture.
Any material, any
idea without hindrance
born into space,
I consider sculpture*"

Isamu Noguchi

Translucent paper, bamboo ribs,
metal rods, wire. Noguchi with
his Akari lanterns in the 1960s.

Akari Lantern 1951
Isamu Noguchi

When artist Isamu Noguchi created his lanterns, he expressed the harmony and balance of his cultural background—he was born in the United States to an American mother and a Japanese father. During the 1950s, he spent a lot of time traveling in Japan. In 1951, after visiting the town of Gifu, where lanterns and umbrellas are made from mulberry-bark paper and bamboo, he designed several lamps, which he called Akari, meaning "light as illumination." His inspiration also came from the lanterns that provided light for night fishing on the Nagara River, and he aimed to replicate their sense of weightlessness.

Noguchi referred to his Akari lanterns as "illuminated sculptures." Their plain, origami-like, abstract shapes blended Japanese art, crafts, manufacture, and design with ideas from contemporary Western art and design. The lamps were produced in a factory at Gifu, using traditional methods. This involved stretching paper over bamboo ribs, metal rods, and wire. Noguchi worked as Constantin Brâncusi's assistant in Paris from 1927 to 1929. The simple, minimalist lines that characterize the Romanian sculptor's work can be detected in Noguchi's lamps. A sculptural note is also evident in Noguchi's furniture and garden designs.

Madam Ruby
Celina Clarke and Simon Christopher 1994

Estação da Luz
Luciana Martins and Gerson de Oliveira 1995

Generation Two Lights
Roland Simmons 1995

Loto Floor and Table Lights
Guglielmo Berchicci 1997

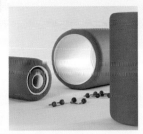

Colombo was fascinated by the changes that were occurring throughout society during the 1960s, and his tube chair design fulfilled his aim to create a "residential unit" of furniture that was both flexible and functional. All the components were designed to fit into a canvas bag which made the entire chair portable, and they could be assembled easily by users. Each padded tube was formed from a single piece of plastic in different colors and sizes, and the cylinders could be clipped together with sturdy metal hooks. Colombo wanted to create "dynamic pieces of furniture" for his "habitat of the future," and designed several "kits" to suit a variety of needs.

Inspired by modernism, Italian architect and designer Joe Colombo responded to changing social conditions after World War II by reinventing furniture and creating innovative interior environments. Using a new process of molding plastic, he designed his tube chair: an adaptable, stylish item of furniture unlike anything seen before, although it was never made for the public. The modular components —cylinders of different diameters—of the foam-covered, lightweight chair could be arranged in any combination, even inserted one inside the other, yet always created an illusion of harmony and unity.

[Furniture should be] autonomous, independent . . . coordinated, and programmed to adapt in any spatial situation, in the present or future."
Joe Colombo

PVC plastic, tubular steel, rubber, polyurethane foam, synthetic knit upholstery.

Donna Up5 Chair
Gaetano Pesce
1969

Torso Chair
Paolo Deganello
1982

Soft Heart Chair
Ron Arad
1990

(Traditionally) leather, goatskin lining, gilt metal. Birkin bags are made in a variety of sizes and colors.

Birkin Bag 1984
Jean-Louis Dumas

Named after the actress and singer Jane Birkin, the Hermès Birkin bag was inspired in 1981. Birkin was seated next to Hermès chief executive Jean-Louis Dumas on a flight from Paris to London when her basket fell out of the overhead compartment, spilling its contents over the floor. Watching her pick up her belongings, he remarked that she should have a leather bag with pockets. Birkin answered: "The day Hermès makes one with pockets, I will have that," to which Dumas replied: "But I am Hermès and I will put pockets in for you." In 1984, Dumas presented her with a black leather bag based on an Hermès design from 1892. The Birkin bag has since become a classic, associated with wealth, materialism, and celebrity culture. Using the company's signature saddle stitching, developed in the nineteenth century, each bag is meticulously made by artisans and takes several days to finish. Since they are individually made, no two bags are the same, and the time that it takes to make each one has added to their perceived desirability.

Amply proportioned Birkin bags are produced in various skins, including calf, goat, and crocodile. Although Hermès has no logo for the Birkin bag, there are certain aspects that distinguish it from other bags, including the flap that extends from the back over the top, a wraparound "belt" that hooks onto the front, and a plated clasp, lock, and key. The Birkin bag is one of the most recognized handbags in existence.

Speedy Bag
Georges Vuitton
1932

2.55 Handbag
Gabrielle "Coco" Chanel
1955

Lady Dior Handbag
John Galliano
1995

Bowling Bag
Prada
2000

Lockheed Lounge 1986
Marc Newson

Newson made the Lockheed Lounge by hammering hundreds of aluminum panels onto a homemade fiberglass mold. By blatantly leaving on show its materials and manufacture in this way, he maintained the object's integrity. The streamlined appearance echoes designs of the 1930s and sculptures by artists such as Jean Arp, Alexander Archipenko, and Karl Hartung. After exhibiting the LC1 prototype, Newson reshaped it into a more flowing form, and, in 1986, named it the Lockheed Lounge after the U.S. aircraft manufacturer.

Loosely based on the chaise longue in *Portrait of Juliette Récamier* (1800) by Jacques-Louis David, the long silver chair by Marc Newson embodied the Australian designer's vision of "a fluid metallic form, like a giant blob of mercury." Made from shiny industrial aluminum, bent and riveted into a curvaceous shape, the Lockheed Lounge recalled Newson's studies in jewelry design and sculpture. An early version of the chair, the LC1, was first displayed in a Sydney gallery in 1984, and photographs of the distinctive piece of furniture featured immediately in magazines all over the world. Madonna affirmed its timeless glamour when she stretched out on one in her video *Rain* in 2006.

I think it's really important to design things with a kind of personality."
Marc Newson

Aluminum, fiberglass, polyester resin, polyurethane. The sheets are joined almost seamlessly.

TV-Relax Chair
Luigi Colani
1969

Tomato Chair
Eero Aarnio
1971

Maralunga Chair
Vico Magistretti
1977

Copper Shade 2005
Tom Dixon

Copper and its alloys have been an essential material for many civilizations throughout history, and they continue to be used in important technologies. Dixon's use of copper in all its purity was innovative and evocative; the mirrored sphere of the copper shade recalled disco balls of the 1970s. Resembling floating bubbles as they hang, his Void Light shades (left) were inspired by Olympic medals.

Self-taught Tunisian-British designer Tom Dixon started his career by making welded furniture. In 2005, he began working with copper to create a range of products that exploited the metal's warm, glossy appearance while drawing on historical associations that had fallen out of favor. In his copper shade, the most popular item in his copper collection, the reflective surface is enhanced by its spherical shape and emphasized by the light shining through it. Created with a thin layer of pure copper fixed to the internal surface of a polycarbonate globe, the light emits either a soft, metallic glow or is bright and vibrant, depending on the light bulb used inside. The shade can be hung singly in a dramatic statement or at different heights in a sparkling cluster or cascade.

> *It was only when people started to buy that I realized I had hit on a form of alchemy . . . I could turn a pile of scrap metal into gold."*
>
> **Tom Dixon**

Plastic polycarbonate pendant globe, clear cable, metallized copper finish.

Havana Hanging Lamp
Joseph Forakis
1993

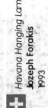

UFO Hanging Light
Nick Crosbie
1996

DESIGNERS

Verner Panton (center) exhibits his furniture designs in Frankfurt (1964).

Alvar Aalto

Hugo Alvar Henrik Aalto (1898–1976) studied at Helsinki Institute of Technology from 1916 to 1921, and established his architectural practice in Jyväskylä, Finland, in 1923. During the late 1920s and early 1930s, he and his wife, Aino Marsio (1894–1949), also a designer, spent time in Europe absorbing the latest trends in modernism, which Aalto adopted—and adapted. Throughout his career, he has produced minimalist buildings, furniture, and other items, using natural materials.

» *Savoy Vase* p.43
» *L-legged Stacking Stool* p.65

Ron Arad

Israeli-born Ron Arad (1951–) studied at Bezalel Academy of Arts and Design from 1972 to 1973, and, in 1979, graduated from the Architectural Association in London. With Caroline Thorman, he founded an architecture and design firm, Arad Associates, in London in 1989. His avant-garde designs include buildings, individual objects, and items for mass production, such as carbon fiber armchairs, polyurethane bottle racks, perfume bottles, and crystal chandeliers.

» *Bookworm Shelf* p.51

Egmont Arens

From 1917 to 1923, Egmont Arens (1889–1966) ran a bookstore in Greenwich Village, New York City. He began publishing at the back of the store from 1918 using a hand-operated printing press. He produced journals, books, and art prints, and later became a leading designer of packaging, plastics, and industrial items. In 1935, Arens founded his own company and designed a range of consumer goods, including toys, cigarette lighters, pens, watches, and kitchen appliances.

» KitchenAid Food Mixer p.113

Charles Robert Ashbee

Designer, writer, and social reformer Charles Robert Ashbee (1863–1942) became a leader of the English Arts and Crafts Movement at the end of the nineteenth century. After graduating from Cambridge University, he trained as an architect, but, in 1887, he founded the School of Handicraft to revive craft techniques and skills that had been supplanted by mass production. In 1904, Ashbee opened the School of Arts and Crafts, specializing in hand-crafted products.

» Decanter p.39

Oskar Barnack

Born in Germany, optical engineer, mechanic, and industrial designer Oskar Barnack (1879–1936) worked as head of microscope research for German manufacturer and optician Ernst Leitz from 1911. Barnack was also an enthusiastic photographer, but he suffered from asthma, and contemporary cameras were too heavy and bulky for him to use. From 1913, he led the camera department at Leitz and developed the smallest and lightest 35mm camera to date.

» Leica Camera p.165

Bausch & Lomb

John Jacob Bausch (1830–1926) and Henry Lomb (1828–1908) emigrated to New York from Germany in 1849. In 1853, Bausch opened a store selling spectacles and thermometers, as well as field, opera, and magnifying glasses. He made spectacle frames from Vulcanite rubber, which was more practical than the usual gold or horn. Lomb, a cabinetmaker, invested in the store and took charge of sales, while Bausch concentrated on manufacturing.

» Ray-Ban Aviator Sunglasses p.137

Harry Beck

London-born Henry Charles Beck (1902–1974) was an engineering draftsman at the London Underground signals office. Curious about the problems that London Transport was having with the development of a map for the various subway routes, Beck produced a design in his spare time, basing it on electrical signal circuits. Although he left London Transport in 1947 to teach typography and color at the London School of Printing, Beck made a number of revisions to the map until 1960.

Alfonso Bialetti

After emigrating to France from Bologna in Italy, Alfonso Bialetti (1888–1970) worked as a smelter until 1918 and then returned to Italy. In 1919, he opened a foundry in Crusinallo in Verbania, producing semi-finished aluminum products, but he soon transformed the workshop into a studio to design and produce more saleable, finished consumer goods. In 1933, he invented his revolutionary coffee maker, the Moka Express. His grandson is the designer Alberto Alessi.

George G. Blaisdell

After being unexpectedly dismissed within two years of enrolling at a military academy, Pennsylvania-born George G. Blaisdell (1895–1978) worked in his family's business: the Blaisdell Machinery Company. Later, he founded a business manufacturing the Zippo lighter, initially employing only three people. As the business strengthened, Blaisdell acquired several buildings as well as great wealth and respect. He went on to become a noteworthy philanthropist.

Marcel Breuer

In 1920, Hungarian-born Marcel Breuer (1902–1981) won a scholarship to study at Vienna Academy of Fine Arts, but he left and studied instead at the Bauhaus in Germany. After graduating, he ran the Bauhaus furniture workshop and co-founded a firm to produce his furniture. From 1928 to 1935, he worked in Berlin, Switzerland, and London, and, in 1937, he emigrated to the United States. There, he became a Harvard professor and formed an architectural practice with Walter Gropius.

George Carwardine

Vehicle designer and engineer George Carwardine (1887–1948) owned a factory in Bath, England, which developed vehicle suspension systems He invented a spring mechanism, which could be moved with ease yet held firm in any position, and, In 1932, he patented a lamp design that featured the innovative spring mechanism. At first, he manufactured the lamp in his own workshops, but, in 1937, he sold the license to Norwegian designer Jacob Jacobsen.

>> *Anglepoise Lamp* p.115

Achille Castiglioni

An Italian master of industrial design, Achille Castiglioni (1918–2002) studied architecture in Milan, and, in 1944, joined the design studio run by his brothers, Livio and Pier Giacomo Castiglioni. Inspired by mundane objects, Achille made use of ordinary materials to create items with maximum impact. He also taught at the Polytechnic University of Turin and at the faculty of architecture at Milan Polytechnic. He won several awards, including the Compasso d'Oro.

>> *Arco Lamp* p.141

Pier Giacomo Castiglioni

After gaining a degree in architecture in Milan in 1937, Pier Giacomo Castiglioni (1913–1968) collaborated with his brother, Livio, and Luigi Caccia Dominioni in a design practice. He was joined by his other brother, Achille, in 1944. Pier Giacomo collaborated with Achille on many original and functional designs, and their lighting for Flos was particularly successful. Their work has been honored by a permanent exhibition at the Museum of Modern Art in New York.

>> *Arco Lamp* p.141

Gabrielle "Coco" Chanel

Gabrielle Chanel (1883–1971) grew up in an orphanage in Saumur, France, where she learned to sew. During a brief career as a singer, she was nicknamed "Coco," but, in 1910, a wealthy boyfriend, Arthur "Boy" Capel, paid for her to rework ready-made hats as a milliner in Paris. From 1913 to 1919, she opened fashion salons in Deauville, Biarritz, and Paris. Chanel opposed prevailing trends, using elements from menswear, emphasizing comfort, and liberating women from restrictive corsets.

>> *Chanel No.5 Perfume Bottle* p.61

James Chesterman

In 1820, James Chesterman (1792–1867) moved to Sheffield to start a business using local steel. Nine years later, he patented a spring device used to rewind measuring tapes automatically. Adopting a bow as his trademark, he named his factory in Nursery Street the Bow Works. In 1842, together with a colleague, James Bottom, he patented a woven cloth tape reinforced with wire strands. Later, he also patented a process for heat-treating steel strips for tape measures.

» *Automatic Tape Measure* **p.73**

Albert Cheuret

French sculptor and designer Albert Cheuret (1884–1966) studied under Jacques Perrin and Georges Lemaire. By the age of twenty-three, he was exhibiting sculpture at the Salon des Artistes Français alongside artists such as Auguste Rodin. Soon he began to design furniture inspired by Art Nouveau and Art Deco styles, including tables, chairs, and lighting. For the Paris Exposition in 1925, dedicated to the modern decorative arts, he designed an entire store.

» *Table Clock* **p.185**

Thomas Chippendale

Cabinetmaker and furniture designer Thomas Chippendale (1718–1779) moved from Yorkshire to London in 1748. He opened a workshop on St. Martin's Lane, a fashionable area for bespoke furniture, and attracted many wealthy clients. Chippendale furnished grand houses throughout Britain, and his illustrated pattern book, *The Gentleman and Cabinet-Maker's Director* (1754), established him as one of the most influential furniture designers of the eighteenth century.

» *Corner Cupboard* **p.19**

Godtfred Kirk Christiansen

The childhood of Godtfred Kirk Christiansen (1919–1995), third son of Ole Kirk Christiansen, was relatively poor. In the 1930s, he began to work with his father, making wooden products, including toys, and was extremely energetic in his efforts to attract sales. After Ole bought an injection-molding machine in 1947, Godtfred came up with the idea of making toy bricks that clicked together. In 1950, Godtfred was made junior vice president of the Lego company.

» *Lego®* **p.97**

Ole Kirk Christiansen

Ole Kirk Christiansen (1891–1958) was a carpenter. He first worked in Germany and then Norway, returning to his native Denmark in 1916, when he bought a workshop in Billund. From there, he built houses in the summer and furniture in the winter. When the Great Depression started to affect business in the 1930s, Ole began making more saleable stools, stepladders, and wooden toys. The "stud-and-tube coupling system" used to fix together Lego bricks was patented in 1958.

» *Lego® p.97*

Clarice Cliff

Born in England, Clarice Cliff (1899–1972) was the fourth of eight children. At the age of thirteen, she became an apprentice enameler. Four years later, she joined A. J. Wilkinson's Royal Staffordshire Pottery as a lithographer, and in 1924 took evening classes at Burslem School of Art for a year. After studying sculpture at the Royal College of Art, Cliff set up a small studio in Wilkinson's Newport Pottery, decorating traditional whiteware with bold designs that appealed to Art Deco enthusiasts.

» *Crocus Crockery p.33*

Wells Coates

Born in Tokyo, Wells Coates (1895–1958) studied engineering in Vancouver, Canada, and graduated in 1921. In Britain, he studied for a doctorate in engineering from 1922 to 1924, and then worked as a journalist in London and Paris. From 1928, he began to design fabrics, furniture, household products, and buildings, adhering to Le Corbusier's modernist principles. His designs for EKCO Radio Company made him one of the most significant designers of the interwar period.

» *EKCO AD 65 Radio p.167*

Joe Colombo

After studying painting and, later, architecture in Milan, Cesare "Joe" Colombo (1930–1971) took over the family business, manufacturing electrical equipment, in 1959 when his father died. In 1962, he opened his own design practice, focusing at first on architectural and interior design projects, and later attracting commissions from a range of prestigious clients, including Alessi, Kartell, and Alitalia. Colombo was a prolific designer when he died at the age of forty-one.

» *Tube Chair p.189*

C

Earl R. Dean

Of English, German, and French descent, Earl R. Dean (1890–1972) began working for the Root Glass Company in Indiana at the age of fourteen. In 1915, he designed the innovative glass Coca-Cola bottle, although he was not recognized for it during his lifetime. In the 1930s, anxiety across Europe adversely affected business for the Root Glass Company, and it was acquired by another company in 1938. Dean moved to a branch in Ohio, and later, briefly, to one in Pennsylvania.

>> *Coca-Cola® Bottle* p.181

James Dewar

James Dewar (1842–1923) was educated in Edinburgh and became a highly influential scientist. At the University of Cambridge, he was made professor of natural experimental philosophy, and at the Royal Institution a professor of chemistry. His research covered a broad field, but it was his investigation into the behavior of substances at low temperatures that made him particularly well known and resulted in his invention of the vacuum flask, or Dewar flask.

>> *Vacuum Flask* p.81

Tom Dixon

A self-taught British designer specializing in welded furniture using recycled materials and industrial scrap, Tom Dixon (1959–) was born in Tunisia. In 1997, he was made head of design for the British Habitat furniture stores and also for Finnish furniture manufacturer Artek. His unrestricted, innovative ideas continue to combine creative solutions with commercial enterprise. In 2000, Dixon was appointed an Officer of the Order of the British Empire for services to British design.

>> *Copper Shade* p.195

Christopher Dresser

Having trained at the Government School of Design in London, Christopher Dresser (1834–1904) began to design professionally from 1858 and became a key figure in the Aesthetic Movement. Believing that designers should stylize botanical forms rather than copy directly from nature, he designed wallpapers, textiles, ceramics, furniture, metalwork, and glassware. Following a trip to Japan in 1876, his work became more minimalist, typical of the Anglo-Japanese style.

>> *Tureen and Ladle* p.23

Henry Dreyfuss

After training at the Ethical Culture School in New York, Henry Dreyfuss (1904–1972) worked as a consultant at Macy's department store and was apprenticed to the industrial and theatrical designer Norman Bel Geddes. In 1929, he opened his own design office in New York. From 1930, Dreyfuss produced telephones for Bell Laboratories, and also designed two trains for the New York Central Railroad between 1936 and 1940. His range of products was shapely and streamlined.

» *Model 302 Telephone* **p.169**

Jean-Louis Dumas

From 1978 until 2006, Jean-Louis Dumas (1938–2010) was chairman and artistic director of the Hermès group. Born in Paris, he was the great grandson of Thierry Hermès, who established the company in 1837. Dumas was educated at Ecole libre des sciences politiques. After traveling, then working as a buyer for Bloomingdale's department store in New York, he joined Hermès in 1964. He rejuvenated the company, making it more desirable and competitive, and turned Hermès into a luxury brand.

» *Birkin Bag* **p.191**

Charles Eames

After studying architecture at Washington University in St. Louis, Charles Eames (1907–1978) started his own architectural practice in 1930. He moved to Michigan in 1938 to further his studies at Cranbrook Academy of Art. There, he met fellow designer Eero Saarinen, with whom he designed award-winning furniture for New York's Museum of Modern Art. In 1941, he divorced his first wife and married Ray Kaiser. Together they created innovative architecture and furniture.

» *Eames Lounge Chair and Ottoman* **p.49**

Ray Eames

Ray Kaiser Eames (1912–1988) graduated from Bennett Women's College, New York, in 1933, and began studying Abstract Expressionist painting with Hans Hofmann. In 1940, she enrolled at the Cranbrook Academy of Art in Michigan, where she met Charles Eames. After marrying the following year, they moved to Los Angeles, where Ray designed magazine covers. Later, she and Charles designed a wide range of furniture and buildings, and also made short movies.

» *Eames Lounge Chair and Ottoman* **p.49**

Kenji Ekuan

Kenji Ekuan (1929–) graduated from Tokyo National University of Fine Arts and Music in 1955. In 1957, he founded GK Industrial Design Associates, which became GK Design Group. Inspiring international trends, Ekuan's designs are intended to improve life, and he continues to chair several design groups, including the Japan Institute of Design. He is also senator of the International Council of Societies of Industrial Design and dean of Shizuoka University of Art and Culture.

» *Kikkoman Soy Sauce Bottle* **p.101**

Karl Elsener

After serving apprenticeships to surgical instrument- and razor-makers in Paris and Tuttlingen, Germany, Karl Elsener (1860–1918) opened a cutlery business in Ibach, Switzerland, in 1884. This was partly to create employment, as many nationals were emigrating. Within seven years, the company had won a contract with the Swiss army to make pocket knives for soldiers. Elsener used his training experience to create innovative, compact, foldaway knives with tools.

» *Swiss Army Knife* **p.79**

Lothar von Faber

When German entrepreneur Lothar von Faber (1817–1896) took charge of the pencil-making company that had been started by his great-grandfather, Kaspar Faber, he widened its scope. Using powerful marketing, he opened branches of the business across Europe and the United States. Most importantly, he brokered a deal to acquire all the best graphite that was being mined in eastern Siberia at that time. He was appointed councillor of state in recognition of his services to German industry.

» *Faber-Castell Colored Pencils* **p.77**

Peter Carl Fabergé

The son of a jeweler of Huguenot descent, Russian-born Peter Carl Fabergé (1846–1920) trained in St. Petersburg, Frankfurt, and Dresden, and visited Paris and London. In 1870, he inherited his father's business and determined to make it more creative. The House of Fabergé became renowned for its designs, inspired by the opulence of Rococo, the traditions of Russia, the Renaissance, and Art Nouveau. In 1882, Peter Carl was awarded a gold medal at Moscow's Pan-Russian Exhibition.

» *Moscow Kremlin Fabergé Egg* **p.27**

Leo Fender

As a child, Californian Leo Fender (1909–1991) repaired radios in his parents' home. After studying accountancy, he began a career as an accountant, but, in 1938, he borrowed money to open his own radio repair store. During World War II, he started K & F Manufacturing Corporation, with Doc Kauffman, which designed and built amplified guitars. In 1945, Fender began selling his own designed guitar. A year later, he formed the Fender Musical Instruments Corporation with George Fullerton.

» *Fender Stratocaster* **p.171**

Paul T. Frankl

Austrian-born Paul T. Frankl (1886–1958) studied architecture at Berlin Polytechnic and traveled in Europe before relocating to the United States in 1914. Having settled in New York, he found employment as an architect but decided to focus on designing and painting fine art and furniture. In 1922, he established Frankl Galleries and later opened a showroom, Skyscraper Furniture. His refreshing designs helped to shape the specific look of American modernism.

» *Skyscraper Furniture* **p.63**

George Fullerton

George Fullerton (1923–2009) moved to California in 1940. He served in the United States Marine Corps during World War II and later found employment at Lockheed Aircraft as a machinist. Impressed by Fullerton's musical background and technical expertise, Leo Fender invited him to join his company, Fender Musical Instruments Corporation. Fullerton's design innovations helped to create the first affordable mass-produced, solid-body electric guitar.

» *Fender Stratocaster* **p.171**

Max Gort-Barten

A Jewish Swiss-German, Max Gort-Barten (1914–2003) worked as an engineer in Germany. However, as the National Socialist party gained strength, his family decided to send him to work for an uncle in South Africa. He flew first to England, but Britain declared war on Germany and Gort-Barten was interned. When he was released, he was given work in intelligence, then in aircraft production. After the war, he patented his Dual-Light electric fire and named his new company for it.

» *Dualit Toaster* **p.83**

E
F
G

Michael Graves

One of the world's first postmodernists, Michael Graves (1934–) attended University of Cincinnati, Ohio, and later gained a master's degree in architecture from Harvard University. In 1964, he set up his own architectural practice and, in 1969, was acknowledged as one of the "New York Five." This group of architects produced contemporary buildings, including important public commissions. During the 1980s, Graves also designed a range of domestic products.

>> *Whistling Tea Kettle* **p.103**

Jacques Gruber

After studying in Paris at two art schools and at the studio of Gustave Moreau, Jacques Gruber (1870–1936) moved to Nancy to be at the forefront of French Art Nouveau. He taught at the Ecole des beaux-arts there, and also produced numerous items for local design companies, particularly glassware. In 1897, he set up his own workshop, making many individual objects as well as stained glass windows, roofs, and canopies for important buildings. He moved to Paris in 1914.

>> *Lily Pond Window* **p.41**

Neville Heeley

As a young man in Birmingham, England, Neville Heeley (1834–1911) joined his grandfather's steel toy making company, James Heeley and Sons. With his father, Francis, Neville manufactured steel toys, as well as "snuffers, boot hooks, button hooks, and nut cracks." James Heeley had started the business in 1815, and, by 1837, corkscrews had been added to the list of steel items it produced. In 1888, Neville created the most successful mechanical corkscrew in history.

>> *A1 Double Lever Corkscrew* **p.111**

Poul Henningsen

Although Danish-born Poul Henningsen (1894–1967), known as PH, studied architecture between 1911 and 1917, he never graduated. A self-taught designer, he opened an office in Copenhagen in 1919. From there, he designed several houses, part of the Tivoli Gardens and two theater interiors. He also wrote articles, theater reviews, poems, and plays. An astute art, architecture, and social critic, he was, however, best known for his unique, glare-free lamp designs.

>> *PH Artichoke Lamp* **p.99**

Walter Hunt

Walter Hunt (1796–1859) obtained a degree in masonry and then worked as a farmer in the mill town of Lowville, New York, where he devised machinery for local mills. After moving to New York City to work as a mechanic, he was granted patents for several inventions, including a fountain pen, knife sharpener, velocipede, safety pin, and ice plow. In 1833, he invented the first workable sewing machine, but, fearing it would create unemployment, he never obtained a patent for it.

» *Safety Pin* p.75

Frederick Hurten Rhead

After an apprenticeship in the English Staffordshire potteries, Frederick Hurten Rhead (1880–1942) worked for various ceramicists. In 1902, he emigrated to the United States and found employment as a potter in Ohio. Seven years later, he began teaching at the People's University in Missouri. He was hired as art director of Homer Laughlin China Company in West Virginia in 1927. While there, he designed his original and colorful Fiesta dinnerware, building on fashionable Art Deco styles.

» *Fiesta Dinnerware* p.135

Maija Isola

Maija Isola (1927–2001) studied painting at Helsinki Art School from 1946 to 1949, and was then hired as a textile designer by Printex, a Finnish textile company. From 1951, she worked for Marimekko, where she was soon made principal textile designer. Drawing inspiration from traditional folk art, modern art, nature, foreign travel, and new, colorful, synthetic dyes, her stylized designs gained popularity throughout Europe and the United States from the 1960s onward.

» *Unikko Fabric* p.175

Jonathan Ive

Having studied industrial design at Newcastle Polytechnic, England, Jonathan Ive (1967–) worked for London-based design consultancy Tangerine, creating a range of products. Aware of the blandness of computers and related products, he joined Apple in 1992 and was soon promoted to director of design. In 1997, he was made senior vice president of industrial design. Ive continues to create a strong brand identity for Apple products and to win many awards.

» *iPhone* p.69

G
H
I

Arne Jacobsen

Before studying architecture at Royal Danish Academy of Fine Arts, Copenhagen, Arne Jacobsen (1902–1971) apprenticed as a mason. Influenced by Le Corbusier, Ludwig Mies van der Rohe, and Walter Gropius, Jacobsen collaborated with Flemming Lassen, a fellow Dane, in 1929, and won a competition for his design for the "House of the Future." In 1930, he established his own office and continued to create timeless buildings and industrial designs throughout his career.

» *Ant Chair* **p.47**

Pierre Jeanneret

Swiss architect Pierre Jeanneret (1896–1967) worked with his cousin, Le Corbusier, for much of his career. In 1926, they published "Five Points of Architecture," which recommended building with roof terraces, continuous windows, supporting columns, plain facades, and no internal walls. In 1929, with Charlotte Perriand, they exhibited steel furniture at the Paris Salon d'Automne. From 1950 to 1965, Jeanneret designed buildings in Chandigarh, India.

» *LC4 Chaise Longue* **p.131**

Nobutoshi Kihara

Nobutoshi Kihara (1926–2011), a Japanese engineer, is best known for developing videotape recording technology. After graduating from Waseda University in 1947, he was employed at Sony Corporation, where he worked on a variety of recording technologies, including magnetic and portable tape recorders, music stereo systems, digital cameras, and transistor radios. In the late 1950s, he designed the first videotape recorder for home use, and, in the 1970s, the Sony Walkman.

» *Sony Walkman* **p.159**

Perry King

Perry King (1938–) studied industrial design in Britain and moved to Italy in 1964, where he found employment as a consultant for Olivetti. His best-known design is the Valentine typewriter with Ettore Sottsass. King moved to Corporate Image, where he designed fonts, books, and posters with Santiago Miranda, with whom he founded King Miranda Associati in 1976. He also taught at Milan University of Technology and at London School of Architecture and Design.

» *Valentine Portable Typewriter* **p.177**

René Lalique

René Lalique (1860–1945) studied jewelry design in Paris with Louis Aucoc and took evening classes at Ecole des arts décoratifs. He also studied at London's Crystal Palace School of Art Sydenham. On his return to Paris, Lalique designed jewelry for companies such as Cartier and Boucheron. In 1890, he opened his own business, designing and making Art Nouveau jewelry and other glass pieces, including items for art dealer Samuel Bing's new store, Maison de l'Art Nouveau, in Paris.

» Bacchantes Vase **p.31**

Edwin H. Land

Before completing his degree at Harvard University, Edwin H. Land (1909–1991) spent time in New York City, where he worked on inventing an inexpensive filter that could polarize light. After returning to Harvard in 1932, he established the Land-Wheelwright Laboratories with his physics teacher, George Wheelwright, to develop the commercial potential of his polarizing technology. He gained funding from investors, and renamed the company Polaroid Corporation in 1937.

» Polaroid Land Camera Model 95 **p.85**

Le Corbusier

Charles-Edouard Jeanneret-Gris (1887–1965), known as Le Corbusier, was a Swiss-French architect, designer, painter, urban planner, writer, and pioneer of modernism. After studying in Switzerland, he worked in Vienna, Berlin, and Paris, where he settled in 1917. Over five decades, he created buildings in the United States, Europe, and India, believing that good design would improve living standards for all. His furniture designs and urban planning followed his modernist beliefs.

» LC4 Chaise Longue **p.131**

Le Creuset

In 1924, two Belgian industrialists, Armand Desaegher and Octave Aubecq, specialists in casting and enameling respectively, decided to amalgamate their expertise. The following year, they set up a foundry in Fresnoy-le-Grand, France, where they produced a unique range of cast iron and enamel cookware based on ancient, robust cooking vessels. By the 1950s, the Le Creuset range had expanded and the products were being exported all over the world.

» Enameled Cookware **p.145**

J
K
L

John Lobb

In the mid nineteenth century, John Lobb (1829–1895) was apprenticed to one of London's leading bootmakers. On completing his apprenticeship, Lobb sailed for Australia, where he made gold rush prospectors hollow-heeled boots for storing their gold. In 1863, he sent a pair of his boots to the Prince of Wales, who appointed him his personal bootmaker. Lobb returned to London and opened his first store producing bespoke shoes in 1866. A Paris store followed in 1902.

» *Half Brogue Oxford* **p.117**

Raymond Loewy

In 1919, after studying in Paris and serving in the French army in World War I, Raymond Loewy (1893–1986) emigrated to the United States. He worked as a window dresser in department stores and as an illustrator for *Vogue*, *Harper's Bazaar*, and *Vanity Fair*. His radical ideas led to commissions to design a vast range of packaging and industrial goods, including logos, a Greyhound bus, Coca-Cola vending machines, Lucky Strike cigarette packaging, and railroad designs.

» *Pencil Sharpener* **p.153**

Dietrich Lubs

Born in Germany, Dietrich Lubs (1938–) studied ship building and, from 1962, trained as a designer at the electronic appliance firm Braun in Kronberg. The design team was led by Dieter Rams, and the two men worked together, creating products that focused on functionality and geometric lines. Together, they designed some of Braun's most successful products, including clocks, calculators, watches, and radios. Lubs was also responsible for graphic design.

» *ET44 Pocket Calculator* **p.155**

Charles Rennie Mackintosh

Scottish architect, designer, and artist Charles Rennie Mackintosh (1868–1928) studied at Glasgow School of Art in 1883 and was then apprenticed to a local architect. In 1889, he joined Honeyman and Keppie as a draftsman, and, in 1896, won a competition to design a new building for Glasgow School of Art. He created numerous distinctive public buildings and tea rooms, items of furniture, and decorative schemes, and his work has influenced a great many designers.

» *Hill House Ladder Back Chair* **p.25**

Ludwig Mies van der Rohe

After training as a stone mason, German-born Ludwig Mies van der Rohe (1886–1969) moved to Berlin and served an apprenticeship at the practice of Peter Behrens. In 1912, he opened his own studio in Berlin and designed several modernist buildings. After World War I, Mies joined the November Group, aiming to revitalize art and architecture in Germany. He moved to the United States in 1937 and became known as the most influential exponent of the International Style.

» *Barcelona Chair* **p.183**

Montblanc

The Simplo Filler Pen company was established in Hamburg, Germany, in 1906 by banker Alfred Nehemias, engineer August Eberstein, and stationer Claus-Johannes Voss. They made their first fountain pen, the Rouge et Noir, in 1909. The improved Montblanc pen came out the following year, and the company was named for it in 1911. By the 1990s, Montblanc had stores across the world, and its range of products had been expanded to include watches and fragrance.

» *Meisterstück 149* **p.163**

William Morris

Designer, businessman, writer, and political campaigner, William Morris (1834–1896) was the leading figure of the Arts and Crafts Movement in Britain. In 1856, he began working in the architectural office of G. E. Street, where he met Philip Webb, who designed his Red House in Bexleyheath. Morris and his friends made all the furnishings, including murals, tapestries, and stained glass. Shunning mass production, Morris promoted simplicity and beauty in design.

» *Tulip and Rose Fabric* **p.21**

Marc Newson

Having studied jewelry design and sculpture at Sydney College of the Arts in Australia, Marc Newson (1963–) began creating furniture. He was awarded a grant from the Australian Crafts Council and used it to stage an exhibition, which featured the iconic Lockheed Lounge. In 1987, Newson moved to Tokyo, where he worked for design company Idée, and, in 1991, he set up a studio in Paris, designing furniture, watches, interiors, and industrial products. In 1997, he began Marc Newson Ltd.

» *Lockheed Lounge* **p.193**

L
M
N

Isamu Noguchi

After studying premedicine at Columbia University, New York, Isamu Noguchi (1904–1988) trained as a sculptor. In 1927, he was awarded a fellowship and traveled to Paris. Although his skills were recognized, it was not until 1938 that he became known in the United States. Four years later, he set up a studio in New York, from where he created sculpture, furniture, lighting, and ceramics. Working relationships with Herman Miller and Knoll followed, confirming Noguchi as a leading modernist designer.

» *Akari Lantern* **p.187**

Verner Panton

Danish-born Verner Panton (1926–1998) was greatly influenced by U.S. and European design. He trained in architectural engineering at Odense Technical School, then studied architecture at Royal Danish Academy of Fine Arts in Copenhagen. For two years, he worked with fellow Dane Arne Jacobsen, and, in 1955, established his own practice. His revolutionary designs for buildings and furniture, using modern shapes, materials, and color, were admired universally.

» *S Chair* **p.67**

Charlotte Perriand

At the age of seventeen, Charlotte Perriand (1903–1999) enrolled at Ecole de l'union centrale des arts décoratifs in Paris. In 1927, she asked Le Corbusier for a job as a furniture designer, but he refused. However, after seeing the rooftop bar she had created for the Salon d'Automne exhibition, he invited her to join him and Pierre Jeanneret to create a range of modernist furniture. In 1940, Perriand advised the Japanese Ministry for Trade and Industry in Tokyo on industrial design.

» *LC4 Chaise Longue* **p.131**

Giò Ponti

With a degree in architecture from Milan Polytechnic, Giò Ponti (1891–1979) set up an architectural studio with two fellow architects. From 1923 to 1930, he also designed porcelain and ceramics, as well as low-cost furniture for the Rinascente store. In 1928, he founded the monthly design magazine *Domus*, which became highly influential among architects and designers. Ponti was commissioned to design Milan's second skyscraper, the Pirelli Tower (1956), a career highlight.

» *La Pavoni Coffee Machine* **p.119**

Dieter Rams

For forty years, Dieter Rams (1932–), Germany's most important postwar industrial designer, worked for the electronic appliance manufacturer Braun. He started studying architecture at the age of fifteen and concurrently trained as a carpenter. After joining an architectural practice in 1951, he moved to Braun in 1955 as an interior designer, where he became interested in product development. His award-winning, rational designs came to epitomize the Braun philosophy.

» *ET44 Pocket Calculator* **p.155**
» *Braun SK4* **p.173**

Lilly Reich

After an apprenticeship as an industrial embroiderer, Lilly Reich (1885–1947) worked for the Wiener Werkstätte, Vienna. She returned to her native Berlin in 1911, where she worked as a window dresser and furniture and clothing designer. In 1912, she joined the Deutscher Werkbund, moving to Frankfurt in 1924. There, she met Ludwig Mies van der Rohe, and the two collaborated on many projects. With Mies, she took charge of the German section of the Barcelona World Exposition in 1929.

» *Barcelona Chair* **p.183**

Gerrit Rietveld

From the age of eleven, Dutch-born Gerrit Rietveld (1888–1965) learned cabinetmaking from his father. He worked as a draftsman for a Utrecht jeweler from 1906 to 1911, and later set up his own furniture-making business. His most important architectural work, the Rietveld Schröder House (1924), Utrecht, follows his furniture design principles, which emerged from his association with the De Stijl movement. In the 1950s, Rietveld worked on social housing projects.

» *Red and Blue Chair* **p.59**

Bernard van Risenburgh II

Bernard van Risenburgh II (c. 1700–c. 1765) was born in Paris into a family of furniture makers. After training as a cabinetmaker in his father's workshop, he set up his own establishment in 1730 and joined the guild of furniture makers. He designed in the Rococo style, and decorated his work with porcelain plaques, veneers, and wood marquetry. Examples of his work now form part of the Royal Collection, and can also be found in a number of major museums across the world.

» *Console Table* **p.91**

Andrew Ritchie

Andrew Ritchie (1947–) graduated from University of Cambridge with a degree in engineering, before finding employment as a computer programmer for a company that later became part of Marconi. He then worked independently for five years as a landscape gardener. In the 1970s, Ritchie met Bill Ingram, designer of the Bickerton folding bike, who inspired him to make his own. He has received several awards, including the Queen's Award for Enterprise in 1995.

Johan Rohde

Danish painter, designer, sculptor, metalworker, and architect Johan Rohde (1856–1935) first studied medicine before turning his attention to art. He studied fine art and then taught anatomy to artists. From 1904 to 1905, he designed silverware for his own use and commissioned Georg Jensen to make it. Impressed with Rohde's work, Jensen employed him to design more silverware. Rohde also produced furniture, textile, and metalwork designs, inspired by Japanese styles.

Rolex

German watchmaker Hans Wilsdorf (1881–1960) founded Wilsdorf and Davis in London in 1905 to distribute timepieces. Wristwatches were not popular at the time, but, in 1908, Wilsdorf registered the trademark "Rolex" and began making watches in La Chaux-de-Fonds, Switzerland. In 1910, Rolex was the first wristwatch in the world to receive the Swiss Certificate of Chronometric Precision. Since then, Rolex watches have been synonymous with precision and prestige.

Ernö Rubik

In 1967, Ernö Rubik (1944–) studied architecture at the Technical University in Budapest and followed it with a postgraduate course in sculpture and interior architecture. From 1971 to 1975, he worked as an architect, during which time, he created the Rubik's Cube, a unique, three-dimensional puzzle of movable cubes that became an international sensation. The designer received the Commander's Cross with Star Order of Merit of the Republic of Hungary in 2010.

Ettore Sottsass

Although born in Austria, Ettore Sottsass (1917–2007) spent most of his life in Italy. He studied architecture in Turin, and in 1955 began designing for Olivetti, creating some of the company's best-known products. Having rejected prevailing modernist design styles, he became a prominent member of the Radical Design movement in the 1960s and 1970s, and his bold designs for the art collective Memphis helped to inspire a new direction in the decorative arts: postmodernism.

» Valentine Portable Typewriter **p.177**

Philippe Starck

After studying interior architecture and product design at Ecole Nissim de Camondo, Paris, Philippe Starck (1949–) set up his first studio at the age of nineteen. He later became art director at the Pierre Cardin studio, producing many original furniture designs. During the 1970s, he designed independently, particularly nightclub interiors. Having established an international reputation, Starck won commissions from renowned companies, such as Alessi, Samsonite, and Vitra.

» Juicy Salif Citrus Squeezer **p.105**

Swatch

In the 1960s, after years of expensive, hand-crafted, Swiss timepieces being passed down through the generations, an influx of inexpensive digital watches from Asia almost destroyed the Swiss watchmaking businesses. In response, entrepreneur and engineer Nicolas G. Hayek (1928–2010) suggested the production of a watch with fewer parts but the same reliable Swiss movement. Swatch watches were the result: affordable, high-quality, and well-designed Swiss timepieces.

» Swatch Watch **p.87**

Freddie Tavares

By the time he was fifteen, Hawaiian-born Freddie Tavares (1913–1990) was a rhythm guitarist in a local orchestra. At the age of twenty-three, he joined the dance orchestra of the Royal Hawaiian Hotel in Waikiki and toured the United States. During that time, to further his music career, he moved to California, where he met Leo Fender. Impressed by Tavares's understanding of electronics and versatile musical skills, Fender employed him to help design electric guitars.

» Fender Stratocaster **p.171**

Chuck Taylor

Charles H. "Chuck" Taylor (1901–1969) played his first professional basketball game in 1919, when he was seventeen years old and still a pupil at Columbus High School, Indiana. In 1921, he began working at the Chicago sales office of Converse Shoes, where his suggestions to improve its sneaker design were adopted. He went on to become an outstanding sales representative for the company. During World War II, Taylor worked as a fitness instructor for the U.S. Armed Forces.

» *Converse All Star Sneaker* p.93

Michael Thonet

German-born Michael Thonet (1796–1871) was apprenticed to a carpenter, then established a furniture-making workshop in 1819. He began to experiment with bending wood in the 1830s, and produced a number of innovative chair designs. These prompted the Austrian chancellor to invite him to Vienna, where he was granted a patent for his process. In 1849, he established a workshop in Vienna, producing furniture for the imperial court and the mass market.

» *Bentwood Chair* p.57

Louis Comfort Tiffany

The son of a wealthy jeweler, Louis Comfort Tiffany (1848–1933) became a leading practitioner of Art Nouveau. After attending a military academy, he went on to study art in the United States and Europe. In the mid 1870s, he began experimenting with stained glass, and in 1879 set up his first interior design and glass-making company. He produced unique iridescent glass and intricate designs, including lamps and vases. He also established a foundation to award grants to arts and crafts students.

» *Peony Tiffany Lamp* p.29

Louis Vuitton

At the age of thirteen, Louis Vuitton (1821–1892) left behind his provincial life to travel. Arriving in Paris in 1837, he was apprenticed to a Monsieur Marechal, a box maker and packer, which was a highly respectable craft at the time. Shortly after Louis-Napoléon Bonaparte became emperor in 1852, his wife hired Vuitton as her personal box maker and packer. Vuitton produced a trunk that revolutionized luggage design and established Louis Vuitton as a luxury brand.

» *Trunk* p.109

Wilhelm Wagenfeld

Wilhelm Wagenfeld (1900–1990) was one of the most important German industrial designers. In 1914, he was apprenticed to silverware manufacturer Koch & Bergfeld. He studied at the Drawing Academy in Hanau, and also under László Moholy-Nagy at the Bauhaus from 1923. By 1928, he was head of the metal workshop at Bauhochschule, Weimar. He designed for many companies and also taught in Berlin. From 1949, he was based in Stuttgart, designing industrial products.

» *Glass Tea Service* **p.95**

Josiah Wedgwood

At the age of nine, Josiah Wedgwood (1730–1795) worked as a "thrower" in the Staffordshire pottery of his eldest brother Thomas, but, after an attack of smallpox, he had to abandon throwing and learn other aspects of the trade. When Thomas refused him a partnership, Josiah moved to other potteries, finally establishing his own factory in Etruria in 1769. There, new methods of glazing, the fair treatment of employees, and the fair division of labor were his main concerns.

» *Pegasus Vase* **p.37**

Russel Wright

Russel Wright (1904–1976) studied painting at the Art Academy of Cincinnati and sculpture at the Art Students League of New York. In 1924, he began designing theatrical sets and caricature masks, and also produced aluminum bar accessories. In 1930, he set up his own workshop in New York and became well known for his domestic products, which included wooden furniture, cocktail shakers, textiles, and dinnerware, designed in a blend of Art Deco style and functionalism.

» *American Modern Flatware* **p.45**

Sori Yanagi

Sori Yanagi (1915–2011) studied art and architecture at the Academy of Fine Art in Tokyo. He was drawn to a career in design by the work of Le Corbusier and later assisted Charlotte Perriand. After teaching at Bunka Gakuin Institute, Yanagi was awarded first and second prizes in the Japan Industrial Design Contest in 1951. The following year, he founded the Yanagi Industrial Design Institute, where he created both industrial and domestic products as if they were art forms.

» *Butterfly Stool* **p.139**

TIMELINE

1775

Corner Cupboard

Pegasus Vase

Console Table

1800

1825

Le Parfait Jars

1850

Automatic Tape Measure

Safety Pin

Faber-Castell Colored Pencils

Bentwood Chair

Trunk

1875

Tulip and Rose Fabric

Tureen and Ladle

Swiss Army Knife

Vacuum Flask

A1 Double Lever Corkscrew

1900

Hill House Ladder Back Chair

Decanter

Moscow Kremlin Fabergé Egg

Lily Pond Window

Peony Tiffany Lamp

Red and Blue Chair

Converse All Star Sneaker

Cosmos Silver Tea and Coffee Set

Coca-Cola® Bottle

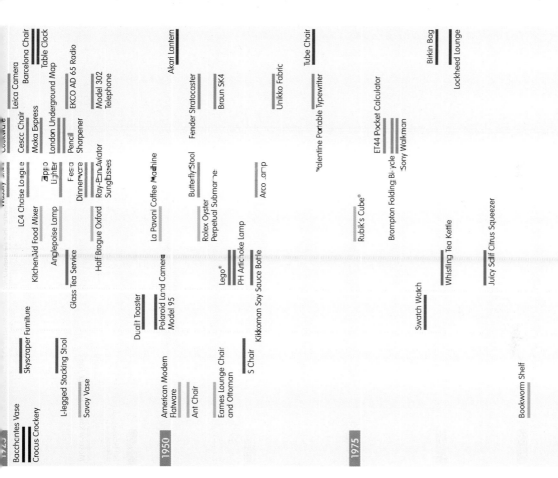

Bacchantes Vase
Crocus Crockery
L-legged Stacking Stool
Savoy Vase
Skyscraper Furniture
Kitchen-Aid Food Mixer
LC4 Chaise Longue
Anglepoise Lamp
Glass Tea Service
Cesca Chair
Moka Express
Zippo Lighter
London Underground Map
Pencil Sharpener
Festa Dinnerware
Half Brogue Oxford
Ray-Ban Aviator Sunglasses
Leica Camera
Barcelona Chair
Table Clock
EKCO AD 65 Radio
Model 302 Telephone

American Modern Flatware
Ant Chair
Eames Lounge Chair and Ottoman
S Chair
Dualit Toaster
Polaroid Land Camera Model 95
Kikkoman Soy Sauce Bottle
Lego®
PH Artichoke Lamp
La Pavoni Coffee Machine
Rolex Oyster Perpetual Submariner
Butterfly Stool
Fender Stratocaster
Braun SK4
Unikko Fabric
Arco Lamp
Akari Lantern
Tube Chair
Valentine Portable Typewriter

Bookworm Shelf
Swatch Watch
Whistling Tea Kettle
Juicy Salif Citrus Squeezer
Rubik's Cube®
Brompton Folding Bicycle
Sony Walkman
ET44 Pocket Calculator
Birkin Bag
Lockheed Lounge

iPhone
Copper Shade

1925
1950
1975
2003

INDEX

Bold type refers to illustrations

AUTHOR

SUSIE HODGE is author of more than eighty books for adults and children, including *How to Survive Modern Art* (2010), *The Great Artists* (2010), *50 Art Ideas You Really Need to Know* (2011), and *Why Your Five-Year-Old Could Not Have Done That: Modern Art Explained* (2012). She has an MA in the history of art and lectures regularly on art and design history in various institutions. Additionally, she writes magazine articles and internet resources for museums and galleries. Susie has also worked for the advertising agencies Saatchi & Saatchi and JWT as a copywriter.

PICTURE CREDITS

9 © Victoria and Albert Museum, London 10 © Christie's Images / The Bridgeman Art Library 11 © PASCAL LAUENER / Reuters / Corbis 12 REX / Jack Nisberg / Roger Viollet 13 © DeAgostini Picture Library / Scala, Florence 14 CAMERA PRESS / JEAN MICHEL TURPIN / Le Figaro Magazine 15 © dpa picture alliance / Alamy 16–17 © Victoria and Albert Museum, London 18 © Victoria and Albert Museum, London 19 © Victoria and Albert Museum, London 20 © Victoria and Albert Museum, London 21 © Victoria and Albert Museum, London 22 © 2013 Digital image, The Museum of Modern Art, New York / Scala, Florence 23 © 2013 Digital image, The Museum of Modern Art, New York/Scala, Florence 24 De Agostini / Photoshot 25 © Derek Harris / Alamy 26 Armoury Museum, Kremlin, Moscow, Russia / Giraudon / The Bridgeman Art Library 28 © Christie's Images / The Bridgeman Art Library 29 © Christie's Images / The Bridgeman Art Library 30 © Bonhams, London, UK / The Bridgeman Art Library 31 © Bonhams, London, UK / The Bridgeman Art Library 32 James Jenkins – Visual Arts / Alamy 33 © Bonhams, London UK / The Bridgeman Art Library 34–35 Digital image, The Museum of Modern Art, New York / Scala, Florence 36 © The Trustees of the British Museum 37 ©The Trustees of the British Museum 38 © Victoria and Albert Museum, London 39 © Victoria and Albert Museum, London 40 DEA PICTURE LIBRARY 41 DEA PICTURE LIBRARY 42 Digital image, The Museum of Modern Art, New York / Scala, Florence 43 Digital image, The Museum of Modern Art, New York / Scala, Florence 44 Digital image, The Museum of Modern Art, New York / Scala, Florence 45 Image copyright The Metropolitan Museum of Art / Art Resource / Scala, Florence 46 © V&A Images / Alamy 47 © G. Jackson /Arcaid / Corbis 48 © V&A Images / Alamy 50 © Victoria and Albert Museum, London 52–53 © Aruldo de Luca / Corbis 54 www.lepurfait.com 55 © Neus Grandia / Alamy 56 Oliver Strewe 57 © Araldo de Luca / Corbis 58 The Museum of Modern Art, New York / Scala, Florence 59 Haags Gemeentemuseum, The Hague, Netherlands / The Bridgeman Art Library 60 © BENOIT TESSIER / Reuters / Corbis 61 © capt.digby / Alamy 62 © The Museum of Modern Art, New York / Scala, Florence 64 © The Museum of Modern Art, New York / Scala, Florence 65 ©The Museum of Modern Art, New York / Scala, Florence 66 Verner Panton 66 Verner Panton 68 © Stefan Solfors / Alamy 69 © dpa picture alliance / Alamy 70–71 REX / James Paterson / Future Publishing 72 © Hugh Threlfall / Alamy 73 © Marc Tielemans / Alamy 74 © Corbis 75 REX / Neville Mariner / Associated Newspapers 76 Courtesy of Faber-Castell USA 77 © Jens Kalaene / dpa / Corbis 78 Victorinox 79 © Myron Jay Dorf / CORBIS 80 © Bettmann / CORBIS 81 © The Royal Institution, London, UK / The Bridgeman Art Library 82 © Dualit 83 © Chloe Johnson / Alamy 84 REX / James Paterson / Future Publishing 85 REX / Jack Nisberg / Roger Viollet 86 © Steve Collins 87 © PASCAL LAUENER / Reuters / Corbis 88–89 © Redfx / Alamy 90 © 2013 Image copyright The Metropolitan Museum of Art / ArtResource / Scala, Florence 91 © 2013. Image copyright The Metropolitan Museum of Art / Art Resource / Scala, Florence 92 © Sergio Azenha / Alamy 93 © Bettmann / Corbis 96 UIG via Getty Images 97 Stephan Zabel 98 © The Museum of Modern Art, New York / Scala, Florence 99 ©The Museum of Modern Art, New York / Scala, Florence 101 © whiteboxmedia limited / Alamy 102 © Elizabeth Whiting & Associates / Alamy 103 © Elizabeth Whiting & Associates / Alamy 104 © Chris Willson / Alamy 105 © Redfx / Alamy 106–107 Copyright Pooch Purtill 108 CAMERA PRESS / JEAN MICHEL TURPIN / Le Figaro Magazine 109 © William Helburn / Corbis 111 © Marilyn Shenton / Alamy 112 © KitchenAid 113 © KitchenAid 114 © Christie's Images / The Bridgeman Art Library 115 John Gay / English Heritage NMR / Mary Evans 116 Copyright Pooch Purtill 117 Copyright Pooch Purtill 118 © Pavoni 119 © Pavoni 120 © ZUMA Press, Inc. / Alamy 121 DANJAQ / EON / UA / THE KOBAL COLLECTION 122 © Digital image, The Museum of Modern Art, New York / Scala, Florence, Rubik's Cube® used by permission of Rubik's Brand Ltd www.rubiks.com 124–125 © Victoria and Albert Museum, London 126 © Peter Harholdt / CORBIS 127 © Peter Harholdt / CORBIS 128 © Victoria and Albert Museum, London 129 agefotostock © snap-fotodesign 132 © funkyfood London – Paul Williams / Alamy 133 MGM / THE KOBAL COLLECTION 134 © ZUMA Press, Inc. / Alamy 135 © ZUMA Press, Inc. / Alamy 136 Mary Evans Picture Library / Epic 137 © David J. Green / Alamy 138 The Museum of Modern Art, New York / Scala, Florence 139 The Museum of Modern Art, New York / Scala, Florence 140 The Museum of Modern Art, New York / Scala, Florence 142–143 © Michele Molinari / Alamy 146 Bequest of Ise Gropius / The Bridgeman Art Library 147 © LOOK Die Bildagentur der Fotografen GmbH / Alamy 148 © Edible images / Alamy 149 © Michele Molinari / Alamy 150 REX / Bournemouth News 151 REX / Bournemouth News 152 © Christie's Images / The Bridgeman Art Library, Images of pencil sharpener and locomotive used with permission of Loewy Design, LLC. www.RaymondLoewy.com 154 The Museum of Modern Art, New York / Scala, Florence 155 Division of Medicine & Science, National Museum of American History, Smithsonian Institution 156 Brompton 157 © I Love Images / Corbis 159 © Roy Morsch / CORBIS 160–161 Getty Images 162 © The Art Archive / Alamy 164 © National Museum of Photography, Film & Television 6 _ 1 7 1 4 / Science & Society Picture Library All rights reserved 165 Jane Brown / Topfoto 166 © Victoria and Albert Museum, London 167 Getty Images 169 Image Courtesy of the Advertising Archives 170 Redferns 171 Redferns 172 akg-images / Interfoto 176 © V&A Images / Alamy 180 JOE HOLLOWAY, JR / AP / Press Association Images 182 De Agostini Picture Library / Scala, Florence 183 © The State Hermitage Museum /photo by Vladimir Terebenin, Leonard Kheifets, Yuri Molodkovets 184 De Agostini Picture Library / The Bridgeman Art Library 185 De Agostini Picture Library / The Bridgeman Art Library 188 Image copyright The Metropolitan Museum of Art / Art Resource/Scala, Florence 190 Chizuko Takagi 191 Chizuko Takagi 192 Private Collection / Photo © Christie's Images / The Bridgeman Art Library 193 Private Collection / Photo © Christie's Images / The Bridgeman Art Library